1001 Ways to Save Money
Thrifty Tips for the Fabulously Frugal!

Wakefield Libraries
& Information Services

ISBN-13:978-1505432534
ISBN-10:1505432537
Cover image courtesy of TheGraphicsFairy.com
All advice is followed at the reader's own risk.

Contents

Kitchen and cooking

1.

Boil vegetables for a short time only, until they are still crisp. This uses less fuel and keeps more of the nutrients intact.

2.

Cheap but bland frozen fish tastes much better if you fry it in a mixture of garlic, rosemary and olive oil.

3.

Serve children ice cream in a cone rather than a bowl; it uses less ice cream and children seem to prefer it.

4.

Make kefir or yoghurt go further for pudding by adding oats and water.

5.

Cheap cream substitute: 1 oz margarine, 1 oz sugar, 1 tablespoon milk powder, 1 tablespoon milk. Mix together well.

6.

Choose sandwich fillings such as peanut butter or hummus which do not require butter.

7.

Don't buy freezer bag clips. Washing pegs or bulldog clips will do the job just as well.

8.

Grate cheese for sandwiches etc instead of slicing it. This uses less and tastes just as good.

10.

Grated carrot is a cheap and healthy way of bulking out meat dishes such as mince, curry etc.

11.

Don't throw away food that's too salty. Try using a little sugar to balance out the taste.

12.

Half a mashed banana with half a teaspoon of baking powder is a cheap substitute for an egg in a recipe.

13.

Dripping (the fat from roasted meat which collects in the roasting dish) makes a delicious spread for toast or sandwiches. Save the dripping in a jar or plastic tub and keep in the fridge.

14.

Have at least one meat free night a week and eat beans, pulses, cheese etc instead. This is cheaper and healthier.

15.

Choose strong cheese if it is not more expensive than mild; the strong flavour means you don't need to use as much of it.

16.

Cut out ready meals and processed foods and cook from scratch. Once you get to know a few recipes it becomes very easy.

17.

Cut out soda pop. You're basically paying for gas, sugar and water.

18.

Remember 'a rotten apple can spoil the whole barrel'. Keep ripe fruit away from less ripe fruit to help the latter last longer.

19.

A pressure cooker uses less fuel and cooks more quickly.

20.

Boil vegetables in the same pot to save fuel and washing up. To avoid things mushing together, use metal pot dividers.

21.

Corned beef is a cheap substitute for mince in spaghetti bolognaise. The fat helps give a rich sauce.

22.

A handgrinder is useful in the kitchen for mincing meat, grinding nuts, stale bread, vegetables etc for cooking; unlike a blender they are inexpensive and don't use electricity.

23.

Creamed tomato (the type available in cartons) with a little salt, garlic and olive oil added makes a cheap and healthy alternative to ketchup and ready-made pasta sauces.

24.

Crumpets with honey make a cheaper alternative to cake at teatime.

25.

Brew your own beer or wine. There are lots of easy recipes on the internet and wine can cost as little as 20 pence a bottle if you use foraged or home grown fruit or vegetables.

26.

A rubber balloon with a pinhole is a cheap substitute for an airlock in homemade wine making. Stretch it over the neck of the demijohn. As the wine ferments it will fill with gas; positive pressure will allow gas out through the pinhole but fresh air cannot come back in. When the balloon goes down completely, fermentation is over.

27.

Cut unsliced bread from both ends alternately. It is said to stay fresher for longer.

28.

Boiling meat usually uses less energy than roasting, and the pot water can be saved for soups.

29.

Check fruit carefully for bruising before buying.

30.

Buy 'bacon bits' for cooking in stews etc. These are cheaper than rashers.

31.

Buy staples in bulk. Things like rice will keep for several months if stored in a large plastic container. Pulses etc can last indefinitely.

32.

Camomile tea makes a cheap alternative to a snack; it's good for the stomach and can make you feel a little fuller.

33.

Bring stale bread back to life by wrapping in a clean damp cloth and warming in the oven for few minutes. (Mouldy bread should be thrown away).

34.

A teaspoon of mustard added to cheese sauce makes it taste stronger, requiring less cheese.

35.

Save the water that potatoes, pasta, rice or vegetables has been boiled in to use as a base for soups. Keep in the fridge for no more than a day or so.

36.

Food close to its sell by date can be bought cheaply from websites such as approvedfood.co.uk

37.

For a cheap alternative to

chocolate spread, simply mix butter and cocoa powder.

38.

Frying is usually the most fuel-economic way to cook.

39.

Drink more water. It fills you up and is good for your body. Sometimes you may think you are hungry when in fact you are just thirsty.

40.

Keep all dried herbs and tea in airtight containers to help them last longer. Even cheap teabags taste better when fresh. Old jam jars are great for free, airtight storage.

41.

Save money on vinegar by making your own. Lots of recipes are available online.

42.

Cook stews etc in bulk to save time and energy; just pop in plastic tubs in the freezer for home made 'ready meals'.

43.

Kefir grains make an economical alternative to yoghurt. The grains are a live culture; you add them to milk and leave them in the fridge overnight where it turns into kefir. The culture lasts indefinitely so they are a good investment. Buy on Ebay for about four pounds.

44.

For cheap crisps (potato chips) use potato peelings. Place on a baking tray and spray a little vegetable or olive oil on them and sprinkle salt also. Bake at 200c for about 10 to 15 minutes.

45.

Keep plastic bread bags tied to preserve freshness. If you make your own bread, wrap it tightly in a clean cotton cloth, but only when it's cool.

46.

Instant mashed potato makes a cheap and quick alternative to 'real' potatoes; they weigh very little and only require boiling water so are perfect for eating in hotel rooms or when camping.

47.

Instant mashed potato can be used to thicken soups, stews etc. Just stir in a small amount while cooking.

48.

Just a small amount of meat such as bacon will give a meaty flavour to frugal dishes of beans, pasta etc.

49.

Keep a supply of powdered milk; that way if you run out of fresh milk you won't have to buy overpriced milk from the local convenience store.

50.

Keep sliced bread in the freezer to preserve it. It can be quickly defrosted or put in the toaster straight away.

51.

Keep the gas flame under the pan. When it comes up the sides it wastes energy and does not heat the pan any better.

52.

Freshen wilted vegetables by soaking them in cold water with a spoonful of vinegar.

53.

Cook to use up what's in your cupboards and what's on special offer in the shops. Avoid celebrity recipes which call for lots of ingredients you don't have.

54.

Kitchen knives can easily be sharpened using a whetstone or knife sharpener. These are cheap and can make dull knives good as new.

55.

Put fruit teabags, such as hibiscus or blackberry, in the pan when making mulled wine, to add body and make it go further.

56.

Fruits such as bananas, apples and peaches should be stored away from other fruit. They emit ethylene, which causes rapid ripening.

57.

When buying garlic, keep individual garlic cloves in the freezer for use when required.

58.

No need to buy an egg yolk separator. Gently squeeze the neck of an empty plastic bottle over the yolk and release. The yolk will be sucked into the neck of the bottle and can be deposited away from the white.

59.

When defrosting items from the freezer, put them in the fridge rather than outside, as it will reduce the amount of electricity the fridge needs to use to keep cool.]

60.

Store potatoes in a dark, breathable cloth bag in the fridge. They will keep much longer in a cool dark place.

61.

Use a pastry brush or clean paint brush to spread butter or margarine instead of using a knife. It uses less and gives better coverage on the bread.

62.

To save money on cooking spaghetti, simply boil water in the microwave and pour into a thermos flask. Add the spaghetti, seal the flask and leave for 30 minutes or so. It will cook in the latent heat within the flask.

63.

Use stale bread in the toaster or for cheese on toast under the grill.

64.

When food or toiletries jars are nearly empty, store them upside down. This will ensure the contents come out more easily.

65.

When using eggs, don't break them all into the same container. Break each one into a mug first; if it's bad you won't have added it to the good ones.

66.

Yoghurt can be made cheaply at home. Warm a pint of milk until almost boiling. Allow to cool to 110F then stir in one tablespoon of live yoghurt. Pour into a thermos flask and leave for 12 hours.

67.

The paper that butter is wrapped in can be used to grease the frying pan or baking trays.

68.

Try the traditional way of serving a roast dinner; serve Yorkshire pudding with gravy first, then meat and vegetables. This way you will feel fuller and will want less meat.

69.

Use masking tape to make labels for fridge and freezer items.

70.

Using loose tea leaves can sometimes work out cheaper than teabags especially with speciality teas such as green tea.

71.

Yoghurt is cheaper if bought in large pots. If you want to take small pots to work, just put it in small jam jars instead.

72.

There are not many good substitutes for instant coffee, but if you prefer an expensive brand, try mixing half and half with a cheaper brand.

73.

Use metal skewers to cook potatoes, meat etc in the oven. This conducts heat into the food, cooking it more quickly.

74.

Weak mulled wine can be strengthened with a few shots of cheap spirits such as supermarket economy brandy.

75.

There's no point spending money on expensive branded spirits to use as mixers. Once tonic, ice, juice etc is added they won't taste much different to the economy brands.

76.

TVP (textured vegetable protein, or soya mince) is a good way to bulk out stews, mince etc with cheap protein.

77.

Wet a kitchen towel and squeeze it out then put in your cake tin to keep cakes fresh.

78.

Three tablespoons of mayonnaise is a cheap substitute for an egg in a recipe.

79.

Two tablespoons of snow (or powdered ice from the freezer) are said to work as a substitute for an egg in recipes.

80.

Use oats to thicken an omelette; you will require fewer eggs.

81.

Use old gingham shirts, tablecloths etc for jam jar lid covers. Make a circular template out of cardboard or use a yoghurt pot lid and draw round it with pencil. Cut out with pinking shears and secure on the jar with a rubber band.

82.

Steaming tea leaves or grinding them before use is said to increase their strength, and thus save on cost.

83.

Switch off the oven for the last 10 minutes or so of cooking time, there will usually be enough heat in the oven to finish the job.

84.

To save money on home-made milk shakes, make the milk go further with a tablespoon of white flour for every pint of milk.

85.

Use a pastry brush or clean paintbrush to salvage all the small bits of fruit, vegetables that collect on a grater after use.

86.

Use the smallest gas or electric ring on the cooker. It will heat all but the largest pans.

87.

When cooking a meal in the oven, put a large metal pan of water in also. This will fill up the space to require less energy for cooking, and can be kept in the oven for washing up water after the meal.

88.

Take butter out of the fridge 30 minutes or so before using it to allow it to soften. If you serve hard butter from the fridge people tend to hack away at it and use much more.

89.

To save on butter, just spread it around the outside edge of the bread, then spread marmalade etc on the unbuttered part in the middle.

90.

Use a rubber spatula to get the last bits of sauce from jars etc. Avoid the cheap inflexible plastic ones sold in pound shops/dollar stores, these are not as good as the rubber ones.

91.

Use up the fat in the frying pan by making fried bread.

92.

The more water you boil, the more fuel you burn. Use the minimum amount of water required to boil vegetables, or better still, steam them.

93.

Toaster ovens, such as the Hinari Tiny Top, are cheap to buy and use much less power than a normal oven. They can be used for all kinds of cooking and are especially useful for single people.

94.

Use leftover or stale wine to make syllabub: For each person mix 1/2 cup sugar, the juice of half a lemon, and 1 cup of whipping cream. Whisk up and add a quarter of a pint of white wine gradually.

95.

Use your local butcher if you have one. The quality of meat will be better than in supermarkets and you can ask about the best cuts to make your money go further.

96.

Stock cubes are cheap and will add meat flavour to an otherwise plain dish.

97.

To make butter go further and spread more easily, beat until soft then add a little hot water (4 tbsp to 8 oz of butter).

98.

UHT milk keeps for a long time unopened and will also last longer than fresh milk in the fridge when opened.

99.

To tenderise tough cuts of meat, rub them with olive oil 24 hours before cooking, and leave in the fridge.

100.

Use stale bread for garlic bread; simply soak in a little olive oil and sprinkle on powdered or fresh garlic, and heat in the oven for a few minutes.

101.

You don't need to keep the power on when boiling eggs. Simply bring the egg to the boil, turn off the heat and cover the pan. Wait five minutes for soft boiled eggs. For hard boiled, boil for two minutes then switch off, cover and wait twenty minutes.

102.

Use ice and soda water to make spritzer from cheap, stale or rough white wine.

103.

You can often use water in mixing a cake instead of milk and the cake will be lighter and less liable to scorch.

104.

Save the fat from meat to use to fry potatoes etc; it gives a very good flavour.

105.

Don't waste stalks or outer leaves from cabbage, broccoli etc. Keep for soup or blend/grate/chop finely to mix in with other food.

106.

Cheap curry can be made with red or green lentils, curry powder and a little olive or vegetable oil. Boil the lentils until they are soft and most of the water is gone, then mix in curry powder and oil. Serve with boiled rice. A cheap and tasty source of protein.

107.

Cheap tea usually improves in taste if you make it in a pot rather than a mug.

108.

Don't throw away stale bread. This can be reused in many ways such as bread and butter pudding, croutons for soups etc.

109.

Freeze leftovers from wine bottles or glasses in ice cube trays in the freezer; these can be defrosted for recipes that require wine.

110.

Don't use tinfoil where clingfilm can be used instead; it is much cheaper.

111.

Crushing tea leaves with a pestle and mortar before use is said to make them taste stronger, thus requiring less tea in the pot.

112.

Save meat or fish bones to make soup. Put bones in a saucepan and cover with water. Add a few lentils, onions or garlic to give body and improve the flavour. Simmer for half an hour or so. Let the mixture cool then pour into a container through a strainer. Using a wooden spoon, work as much of the leftover mixture through the strainer as possible. This is a particularly good way of using up fish leftovers with lots of small bones. If the soup is too thin, thicken it with milk or cornflour.

113.

Change from black tea to green tea. This is healthier, and is drunk without milk, saving you money as well.

114.

Save fuel when cooking rice by soaking the uncooked rice in water overnight – it won't need to be boiled so long.

115.

Most grated vegetables can simply be zapped in the microwave without water. It uses very little power and keeps in a lot of the nutrients.

116.

Save the vinegar from pickled onion jars for cooking, pouring on chips etc.

117.

Save on butter by making it at home, if cream is on special offer in the shops. Pour one pint into a two pint jar or container and seal tightly. Shake vigorously for 10-15 minutes until the buttermilk separates. Pour this off and repeat until butter is formed. If you have a bread machine, check if it has a butter churning programme.

118.

Save money on vegetables with a big bag of frozen mixed veg, which costs about a pound. It's quicker and cheaper than using fresh vegetables which might otherwise be wasted.

119.

Save on greaseproof paper by using the inner bag from cereal packets.

120.

If you buy a bulk stock of perishable items that you use every day, such as teabags, store them in 'short term' and 'long term' containers. The short term container should hold just enough for a week's usage. The long term container therefore only gets opened once a week to top up the short term container, and thus the bulk of the stock stays fresher for longer.

121.

Nettles are a healthy and tasty free food – use them to make soup, tea, or as a substitute for vegetables like spinach. Unlike spinach, nettles won't make your teeth feel odd. Use the tops of the plant only, when young and green. The sting disappears after boiling.

122.

Coffee grounds in a *cafetiere* can be reused once to make weak milky coffee or iced coffee. Don't keep used coffee grounds for more than a day as they moulder quickly.

123.

Couscous is a quick and filling substitute for potatoes, pasta or rice at mealtimes. It doesn't require cooking so saves energy – simply soak it for fifteen minutes in boiling water.

124.

Save money on Indian and Chinese takeaways by cooking the rice yourself at home.

125.

Mix a tablespoon of flour with a little water to make a paste; this will provide a cheap thickener for soups.

126.

Spicy foods with chillis, onions etc will make you feel fuller for longer.]

127.

Semolina is very cheap and easy to make as a filling pudding. Serve with sugar, raisins or grated chocolate to make it more interesting.

128.

Cheap wine poured into a jug from a couple of feet above (beware of splashes) will fill it with oxygen and allow it to 'breathe' which usually improves the flavour – this is common practice in wine-drinking countries such as France, Italy etc.

129.

Cheap, nasty or stale red wine can be turned into delicious mulled wine. To one litre of wine add one dessert spoon of cloves, one dessert spoon of all spice, four tablespoons of sugar and lots of orange and/or lemon rind. Heat up gently in a saucepan.

130.

Serve meat as a side dish rather than a main course. A small amount of highly flavoured meat such as bacon can give a meaty taste to a meal without too much expense.

131.

Always follow recipes carefully. A simple mistake can be costly.

132.

Reuse teabags. On second usage, keep the bag in the mug while you drink, for maximum infusion. This works well with most black teas and herbal teas. Store bags in the fridge and don't keep them for more than a day.

133.

Save money on fruit and vegetables by visiting pick your own farms. There are lots of these across the UK and around suburban London. Take your children and enjoy a frugal day out! It's normally only worth it if you have freezer facilities for storage.

134.

A spoonful of Marmite or Bovril is a cheap way to liven up pasta, rice etc.

135.

Always check eggs carefully before buying to make sure none are cracked.

136.

Always keep the lid on a saucepan when boiling vegetables; it uses less fuel and helps keep flavours trapped inside.

137.

Make butter go further by mixing in margarine or spread.

138.

Make your own fresh bread for pennies in a few minutes, without buying an expensive machine. Just mix 470g of flour, 2 teaspoons of baking soda, a teaspoon of salt, and a dessert spoon of vinegar, a dessert spoon of vegetable oil. Mix together then work in enough water gradually to make it into the consistency of cold ice cream. Put on a floured baking tray and bake for about 40 mins at 170 celsius.

139.

A tablespoonful of vinegar put in the water in which meat is boiling will make the meat tender.

140.

A cheap form of ice cream can be made easily with bananas. Mash a couple of bananas into a plastic box with a little milk and add sugar or honey for extra sweetness. Then leave in the freezer until solid. It's a good way of using up over-ripe bananas.

141.

Soy sauce is an economical way of livening up bland food such as noodles; only a few drops are required.

142.

Save money on oven fuel by using a simmer ring. This is a small metal plate that you can put over your gas hob to allow items to simmer at very low temperatures by diffusing the heat. They are available online for a few pounds.

143.

Revive wilting lettuces by sitting them in cold water for half an hour.

144.

Powdered mustard lasts longer in storage than the made up variety.

145.

Sour fruit can be neutralised and made edible by sprinkling it with bicarbonate of soda.

146.

Milk which is 'on the turn' can be freshened for use in cooking, by stirring in a little bicarbonate of soda.

147 .

A slow cooker will save lots of energy and will soften tough meat.

148.

Skimmed milk is a waste of money. A similar effect can be achieved with less cost by buying full fat milk and diluting it a little. You can do the same with other dairy products such as yoghurt or kefir.

149.

Save the juice from tinned fruit and add soda water to make a refreshing fruit drink.

150.

Save money on kitchen bin liners by using supermarket carrier bags instead.

151.

Pour tea from the pot into the cup a little higher than normal; the added gravity force mixes in air to improve the flavour. This works with cheap wines as well.

152.

Pour a little boiling water into an almost-empty jar of instant coffee and shake to use up the remainder. Add the liquid to a fresh cup of coffee or use for cake flavouring etc.

153.

Many products can be diluted to make them last longer and can even taste better that way. Concentrated fruit juice and mayonnaise, for example, can easily be diluted by up to 50%.

154.

Put broccoli into water, like a bunch of flowers, and store in the fridge. It will keep longer.

155.

Avoid expensive unhealthy crisps and similar snacks. Carrot or celery sticks with dips are cheaper and better for you.

156.

Ask your butcher or fishmonger for any offcuts etc 'for the dog' (or cat!), they will sometimes give meat or fish for very little charge which can make good soups, stews etc.

157.

Produce in-season is usually cheaper than out of season produce.

158.

Save money by making your own ice cream at home. You don't need an expensive machine. Whisk together 2 cups of cream, 1 cup of milk, 14 oz condensed milk, the juice of two lemons, ½ a teaspoon of vanilla extract and a pinch of salt. Put in the freezer in a tub and stir thoroughly every half an hour for three hours until it is the right consistency.

159.

Always save leftovers. They can be used in many different ways. See books such as Frontier Frugal for some tips.

160.

Don't pour old fat down the sink; it can cause serious blockages and big plumber's bills! If you don't use it up for other cooking, put it in an old jam jar and throw it out with the rubbish when full.

161.

Poor man's steak: mix mince with an equal quantity of oatmeal and little olive oil and garlic. Knead it together and form into 'steaks' then fry or grill.

162.

An old wartime tip: don't tell the people you are cooking for what is in the food until **after** they have eaten it!

163.

Airline sick bags make good lunch bags for sandwiches (if unused, obviously!)

164.

If you cook something with peeled apples, keep the skins and put them in the blender to make into fruit smoothies.

165.

Peanuts are full of protein and make a good meat substitute in many dishes. Buy large value packets from the supermarket but rinse off the salt first.

166.

Shredding or grating vegetables helps you cook them quickly in very little water.

167.

Avoid packaged cereals for breakfast. They are expensive and often laden with sugar and other chemical nasties. Oatmeal can be used to make porridge, or eaten raw with dried fruits as muesli. It's cheap, healthy and filling.

168.

Soak cheap meat in vinegar to tenderise it.

169.

Save breadcrumbs from your breadboard. These keep indefinitely and can be used in many recipes. At the very least they can go on the bird table.

170.

Onions are cheap and will liven up any dull or bland food.

171.

A cheap funnel can be made by cutting in half and inverting a plastic water bottle or washing up bottle.

172.

Salad can be made cheaply all year round using grated cabbage, grated carrots and radishes. Add a little mayonnaise or dressing. This will keep longer in the fridge than lettuce.

173.

One and quarter cups of sugar and a third of cup of water is a cheap substitute for one cup of honey in a recipe.

174.

Make home made fizzy pop cheaply using economy fruit juice and sparkling water. Kids love it!

175.

If a single reused teabag doesn't make a strong enough cup of tea, save the bags from two fresh cups to make a third.

176.

A five litre (one gallon) plastic water bottle is a cheap substitute for a glass demijohn in homemade wine making.

177.

Line the vegetable drawer of your fridge with newspaper or kitchen towel. This absorbs moisture and helps vegetables last longer.

178.

A couple of drops of almond essence added to supermarket cola makes a cheap substitute for 'Dr.Pepper.'

179.

If you have a microwave, use it. They use less energy. Vegetables can be steamed easily in a microwave. You can buy a plastic steamer, or just use a glass dish or plate with a little water in it. It's cheaper than boiling on the hob.

180.

Liquids in tetrapacks will keep longer if you seal the opening with a bulldog clip when not in use.

181.

Squeeze teabags in the mug to get the most out of them. You can buy a gadget for this purpose, or just press the bag hard with a teaspoon on the edge of the cup.

182.

Oat flour is cheap and healthy for use in place of wheat flour, and can be made easily by putting porridge oats in a blender.

183.

Parmesan rind can be used in soups to add flavour; just remove before serving.

184.

If you don't make homemade bread very often, buy yeast in sealed packets, not jars or tubs, as this goes off eventually after being opened.

185.

Make grated cheese in sandwiches go further by mixing with grated carrots.

186.

Porridge doesn't need to be made with milk; water will work just as well; or try using half milk and half water.

187.

A tiny pinch of salt makes poor quality tea taste better.

188.

If you eat porridge for breakfast, save on time and energy by soaking the oats in water or milk overnight in the fridge. In the morning just eat them cold or zap them quickly in the microwave.

189.

If you regularly take a packed lunch to work, don't use clingfilm or tinfoil to wrap your sandwiches. Costs add up after a while. Instead, use a plastic sandwich box from a pound shop or the free boxes from Chinese takeaways. It will also stop your sandwiches getting squashed on the way to work.

190.

Avoid sliced meats in plastic packets. These are hugely expensive in terms of weight. Instead, buy cured bacon in packets and slice yourself, this will cost much less and the meat is often better quality.

191.

Add Bovril to soups, stews etc to give a meat flavour without expense.

192.

If you need sausage meat for a recipe, it can be cheaper to buy sausages and extract the meat from the skins, rather than buying it whole.

193.

An extremely cheap meat substitute is *mein chin* or *seitan*, used in Chinese cooking. Mix flour with a little water and salt until it is a doughy ball. Let it stand for two hours, then fill a mixing bowl with water. Knead the dough, changing the water a couple of times, until the dough becomes rubbery. Cut into small pieces and stir fry; it works best if you cook it with real meat so that it absorbs the flavour.

194.

Always keep flour, sugar etc in airtight jars to prevent spoilage. Loose, open paper bags in a cupboard can attract pests like moths. If you don't have enough jars, use a tightly knotted plastic bag.

Beauty and bathroom

195.

Use a soap dish with drainage to allow soap to dry – it will last longer.

196.

Save money on female sanitary items with a 'mooncup'. This is a small reusable sanitary product available cheaply online which has a lot of positive reviews.

197.

Check the fluoride content which is the most important ingredient.

198.

Lemon juice will lighten light brown hair to blonde. Apply to your hair and sit in the sun to dry.

199.

Drinking plenty of tap water is one of the best ways to get healthy looking skin – and it costs almost nothing.

200.

A good quality cut throat razor (open razor) will last a lifetime. They require careful handling (see instructional videos on youtube).

201.

The cheap, unbleached rolls of toilet paper work just as well as the more expensive stuff. If you're worried about what guests might think, keep a roll of good quality paper to put in the bathroom when they come to call.

202.

Children love novelty bubble bath bottles, but it's usually the bottle they like, not the stuff inside, so when it runs out just refill with cheap supermarket bubble bath.

203.

Use an old duvet to lag the outside of your bathtub. This will keep bath water warmer for longer. If you have a panelled bath, nobody will see it.

204.

Save money on hair dye. Morgan's Pomade is inexpensive and darkens the hair gradually; use daily until you get the shade you want then just use once or twice a week to maintain the colour.

205.

Sodium bicarbonate and salt is said to be a good cheap alternative to toothpaste, just dip in your brush and brush as normal. It doesn't contain fluoride, however, which is the active ingredient in toothpaste.

206.

Keep a bucket in the shower or stand in a bowl to catch run-off water; this can then be used to water plants or for cleaning floors, etc.

207.

Cut off the foot of an old pair of tights (pantyhose) to make a small bag. Put in any small slivers of soap that are too small to use. Tie the bag tightly and keep in the shower as a cleansing and exfoliating body scrubber. Make sure you hang it up to dry after use.

208.

A 'cut-throat' razor will last a lifetime, if you invest in a good one. However, these can be tricky to use and can cut more easily.

209.

Use up the last few drops of nail polish in a bottle by adding a drop or two of nail polish remover, closing the bottle and shaking hard.

210.

Use conditioner instead of shaving cream for legs.

211.

Companies such as TapMagic sell small devices that will attach to your taps or shower heads. These reduce water flow but aerate the water, giving the impression of a strong rush without the expense.

212.

Save on lipstick by using a lip brush to apply rather than using the stick.

213.

Vaseline is a cheap alternative to treatments for hard skin. Simply rub on after showering.

214.

The frothed white of an egg is said to make an effective face mask.

215.

Lemon juice, either fresh or from a bottle, can be used as an underarm deodorant; just rub on after washing.

216.

Dye your hair at home. Saves a fortune on salon costs.

217.

A handful of oats in a sock or muslin bag in the bath while you soak will give you a low cost skin-softening treatment.

218.

Used camomile teabags make great eyepads to bring down puffy eyes or reduce bags under the eyes.

219.

Store soap in a dry place for a long time (months or years) before using. It hardens with age and lasts longer when used.

220.

Don't buy washcloths. Simply cut out the unworn parts of old towels with pinking shears. Hem with a sewing machine for extra durability.

221.

A cold shower in the morning saves hot water but can actually make you feel warmer throughout the day, as it stimulates blood flow.

222.

Large bottles of economy bubble bath can be used as a substitute for shower gel and liquid soap.

223.

When buying aqueous cream, choose the cheaper variety which costs around £2 for a tub. The more expensive variety, at about £9 a tub, has a higher oil content but does not work much differently.

224.

To save on shampooing, brush a little baby powder or talcum powder into your hair to absorb excess oil. This costs much less than 'dry shampoo'.

225.

Most pop songs last around three minutes. Play the radio when showering to help you know when to turn off the shower.

226.

Apply body lotion immediately after showering when the skin is still damp; the lotion will go further.

227.

Foundation too dark? Don't throw it away. Add moisturiser to lighten and make it go further.

228.

Use your shower on a setting just warm enough to take the chill off the water. Water that's too hot wastes money and can even be dangerous.

229.

Squeeze loo rolls into an oval shape before putting them on the roller. It makes it more difficult to pull off more than one sheet at a time.

230.

Don't buy expensive hand cleaning products for mechanics, gardeners etc. Simply mix a dessert spoon of vegetable oil with a teaspoon of salt, and work well into the hands. Wipe off with kitchen towel or rags, then wash with soap and water.

231.

A cheap draining soap dish can be made by stretching two or three rubber bands across a saucer or small dish. The soap sits on the bands and drains into the dish.

232.

Keep your razor dry, clean and wrapped up in a cloth when not in use. If you leave it in the shower it will rust very quickly.

233.

If your mascara is nearly out, dip the brush in boiling water, put back in the tube and shake to make it last a little longer.

234.

Cut make up remover pads, sponges etc in half to make them go further.

235.

2 tablespoons of apple cider vinegar to one cup of water makes an inexpensive hair cleanser.

236.

Use the smallest amount of product to get the job done. Manufacturer's guidelines usually tell you to use far more than you need. Experiment to drive costs down.

237.

Soak your toothbrush overnight in neat white vinegar to sterilise and freshen it.

238.

Make razor blades last longer by hand stropping. Simply rub the razor (whilst in the handle) on the palm or your hand (away from the cutting edge) a few times before shaving. You can also do this on an old pair of denim jeans or the inside of a leather belt. This works for both cartridge and double-edged blades.

239.

Adding a little mustard powder to tepid bathwater is said to make it feel warmer and ease muscle soreness. Rinse off immediately if you feel any burning.

240.

Wash hair less frequently to save money on water, hair care products and electricity for the dryer. Washing too often causes hair to lose its natural shine.

241.

To make a shaving brush last longer, dry gently with a towel after use and store upside down to prevent the bristle base rotting. Stands are sold for this purpose but a simple loop of string on a hook will do just as well.

242.

For a cheap facial, put very hot flannels on your face. Impurities will rise out in the steam. Traditional barbers have used this method for many years.

243.

Visit your local beauty college. Many will offer beauty treatments and hairstyling at very low prices.

244.

Three tablespoons of vinegar massaged into your hair before shampooing is said to control dandruff, and is cheaper than anti-dandruff shampoos.

245.

Five crushed aspirins mixed with yoghurt is said to make a cheap and soothing face mask.

246.

Make free hair scrunchies by cutting worn-out tights into horizontal bands.

247.

Use less toothpaste. A pea size amount is all that's required.

248.

Small amounts left in tubes, jars etc? Put a little water in and shake well, then use.

249.

Consider growing a beard to save on razor blades; but remember, it will still need to be trimmed occasionally.

250.

Use olive oil for makeup remover, or a great body lotion after showering.

251.

Soak your shaving brush in equal parts water and white vinegar for a couple of hours; rinse and blow dry; it will soften and revitalise the bristles and will require less soap to lather.

252.

Crystal deodorants are cheaper than roll-ons and last a long time. Some people find they don't work well but they are worth a try.

253.

Save a fortune on haircuts by buying a hair clipper set. These cost about fourteen pounds but will pay for themselves many times over. They are easy to use for simple styles for male family members.

254.

Cheap aftershaves from high street chemists, such as Boots and Superdrug cost considerably less than heavily advertised luxury brands; they do the job just as well.

255.

Use a shaving stick and brush instead of shaving foam. A shaving stick will last about six months, costs much less than foam, is easier to travel with and creates less waste.

256.

Equal parts of conditioner and Epsom Salts is said to act as a hair volumiser.

257.

If your crystal deodorant has become too small to use or you have broken it, soak the pieces in water in a spray bottle and use as a spray on deodorant.

258.

Use a pastry brush or clean paint brush to get the last bits of a twist-up gel deodorant out. Then simply 'paint on'.

259.

Change to a double-edged razor; blades are cheaper than cartridges and can be ordered cheaply in bulk online.

260.

Save £££$$$s by using own-brand petroleum jelly as lip balm and makeup remover . Put some in a small container to carry in your pocket instead of chapstick.

261.

If your aftershave or perfume is not in a spray bottle, decant small amounts into a small spray bottle from a pound shop. This makes it easier to control the amount you use and will keep the scent fresher.

262.

Two teaspoons of bicarbonate of soda in a glass acts as a denture cleaner.

263.

Rub used coffee grounds on your skin in the shower, as a cheap body scrub.

264.

Change shower gel to soap. Shower gel is expensively packaged, mostly water and most of it goes down the plughole anyway.

265.

If you prefer shower gel to soap, pour a small amount on a sponge or shower mitt, it will go much further than if you use your hands.

266.

Vinegar can be used as a cheap alternative to aftershave to disinfect your skin. The vinegary smell should disappear after a few minutes.

267.

There's no need to pay for a styptic pencil to close shaving cuts. The old fashioned method – dab with aftershave and stick a small piece of tissue or loo paper over the cut- is cheap and effective. Remember to take the paper off when the cut has dried; wet the paper before removal to prevent the cut opening when you pull the paper off.

268.

Economy foam bath makes a cheap substitute for handwash in pump dispensers.

269.

A mixture of one teaspoon of sodium bicarbonate to eight ounces of water is said to work as an effective denture soak. Check with your dentist before using.

270.

Limit showers to two minutes to save hot water.

271.

Your local family planning clinic will sometimes give out free condoms.

272.

Red or pink lipstick can double as blusher. Use a tiny amount and rub well in.

273.

Brown sugar and olive oil makes a great cheap exfoliant.

274.

Turn off the water when soaping. Turn the water back on to rinse off. This is called a 'submarine shower' as it's the method used to conserve water on ships.

275.

If you have long hair, use a plughole filter in the bath or shower to avoid blockages and costly plumber's bills.

276.

Wrap your razor tightly in a clean cloth such as an old handkerchief when not in use, and store out of a damp atmosphere, to prevent corrosion and promote longer blade life.

277.

Put pieces of soap too small to use into a liquid soap dispenser with some water and shake occasionally for cheap liquid soap.

278.

Avoid spending on herbal bath essences. Used herbal teabags or eucalyptus leaves in the bathwater will work just as well.

279.

Try shaving with ordinary soap, aqueous cream or olive oil instead of shaving soap, these can work well depending on your beard type and razor. This works for womens' legs as well.

280.

If you colour your hair, save money with a root touch up kit instead of redyeing.

281.

When washing your hands, fill the basin with a couple of inches of water instead of running the tap with the plughole open. After soaping, rinse off with clean water.

282.

Try a flannel soaked in hot water instead of using make up remover.

283.

Pay attention to your feet – long toenails and rough skin can act like chisels and sandpaper on socks and shoe linings.

284.

Growing a few day's stubble is another way to save on blades if you don't want a full beard; stubble is now as conventional a look as being clean shaven.

285.

Avoid manufactured pumice stone blocks, these wear out relatively quickly. A natural stone lasts for many years.

286.

When using a shaving brush, work up the lather in the palm of your hand or in a bowl (any plastic bowl will do; the ones that Christmas puddings come in are good) rather than on your face. The bristles of your beard will wear out the brush more quickly.

287.

Use up the last few drops of perfume in a bottle by adding water to make a body spray or clothes freshener.

288.

Squash loo rolls before putting them on the holder. This will dissuade people from spinning off lots of paper.

289.

Keep a two minute egg timer in the bathroom. This will help you brush your teeth for the right amount of time and will make it easy to keep to a two minute limit in the shower.

290.

Cut open toothpaste tubes or any other container with small amounts left in it.

291.

A cheap cleansing mask can be made from oatmeal and water. Just rub on your face and leave for 30 minutes then rinse off.

292.

When buying toilet paper check cost per sheet and how thick each sheet is. Manufacturers make cheap toilet rolls look thicker by making a bigger hole in the middle of the roll and by bulking out the paper with a pressed on pattern. There's no point buying cheap paper if you need to use double the amount in the loo! Try the squeeze test – hold a multipack of rolls on either side and squeeze together gently; the more 'give' there is, the thinner the paper is.

293.

To squeeze the last bits out of a tube of toothpaste, place the tube on a flat surface then roll over it firmly with the handle of your toothbrush (or any flat hard object) until the contents are squeezed to the top.

294.

Apply lemon juice to age spots to lighten them.

295.

Olive oil can be used as eye makeup remover.

296.

Get a few more uses out of an almost-gone mascara by standing it in a glass of warm water or heating it up with a hair dryer.

297.

Use aqueuous cream for moisturiser, it is cheap and effective and suitable for sensitive skin.

298.

Save money on hair thickening products; if you brush or blow dry your hair while hanging your head upside it will add volume naturally.

299.

Choose a low maintenance hairstyle, such as straight style which only requires the ends to be cut every few weeks. Saves money on hairdressing trips.

300.

Use less deodorant. Instead of 'rolling on', just dab it on.

301.

Save small pieces of soap: they can be stuck to a new bar. Roughen the new bar with a pumice stone or nailbrush, stick the old bit on then turn upside down in the dish so that the weight bonds it as it dries. If you use the same type of soap it won't show.

302.

Condoms are much cheaper bought in bulk online than from high street chemists.

303.

Using two or three inches less water in the bath will save power and money. Use a piece of tape to mark the minimum level you can use in comfort.

304.

To make perfume last longer, rub a little petroleum jelly on your skin, then apply perfume on top.

305.

Most hair products that give shine can be substituted by a little bit of olive oil or petroleum jelly.

306.

After showering, skim the water off your body with your hands and just pat dry with a towel. Vigorous rubbing works skin cells into the towel, which makes it get smelly and need laundering more often, and also wears it out more quickly.

307.

Wet your makeup sponge slightly before using; it will absorb less foundation.

308.

For serious hot water savings try a strip wash at the sink instead of a bath or shower. Rub down with a wet flannel and soap then rinse off; keep showers for when you want to wash your hair.

Clothing, fabrics and jewellery

309.

'Supermend' repair powder can be used for easy fabric repairs. Simply sprinkle on the fabric then iron.

310.

If your pullover sleeves are wearing thin but you don't want to patch them, simply unpick the sleeves from the body and swap the arms over, then resew. This will distribute wear more easily.

311.

Children's trousers which are out at the knees can be repaired with colourful iron on patches of cartoon characters etc.

312.

To make a ring with a stone fit better: attach tiny layers of card and gaffer tape on the underside of the gem, where they won't be seen.

313.

For a permanent version of the above tip, use Milliput modelling clay on the underside of the gemstone. It will set rock hard.

314.

A key and change purse saves wear and tear from coins on pocket linings.

315.

Trousers that have gone at the knees or cuffs can be cut off to wear as shorts.

316.

Preserve the life of leather items (belts, jackets, briefcases etc) by regularly cleaning with saddle soap or balsam. Don't use coloured shoe polish as this can stain clothing.

317.

Choose light colours for summer clothing. This will reflect heat better and will be less prone to fading in the sun, meaning your clothes will last longer.

318.

The inside of a banana skin will give a quick shine to your shoes and works in the same way as those 'instant shoe shine' sponges. Just rub on then buff off with a cloth.

319.

It is said that putting tights in the freezer overnight before their first wear prevents runs.

320.

Never buy a handkerchief or bandanna again. Simply cut up scrap cotton clothing and hem the edges.

321.

Don't throw rubber gloves away when they leak. A blob of glue over the hole (inside) will mend them. A rubber glue such as Shoe Goo is best.

322.

To mend a broken leather belt, lightly glue the two parts together. Once dry, use a little shoe polish or a marker pen of the same colour to cover up any exposed leather on the outside. Then reinforce the back of the belt with layers of gaffer tape cut to size.

323.

A black felt marker (waterproof ink) can be used to touch up scuff marks on shoe heels and small stains on black clothing. Do a spot test first.

324.

Don't remove your belt from your jeans or trousers when you take them off unless necessary, it causes wear on the belt loops.

325.

The sleeves of an unwanted woollen jumper can be reused. Just hem the ragged end and stitch the cuff holes together. Wear as leg warmers/ wellington liners.

326.

Refresh and reshape an old felt or straw hat by steaming it over the kettle.

327.

For everlasting socks - simply patch them with material cut from an old odd sock and stitch on. This works best on holes in the heel area and can provide extra padding for frequent walkers.

328.

A lemon studded with cloves and kept in the wardrobe is said to keep away moths.

329.

Turn duvets and pillows round every time you make the bed. It distributes wear more evenly, making them last longer.

330.

To stop a loose button falling off before you have time to sew it, coat the thread with clear nail varnish.

331.

Faded jeans and denim jackets can be restored to new by using machine dyes such as Dylon Blue Denim.

332.

A heavy shoulder bag can wear out fabric on a jacket quickly, especially if it is a lightweight material like linen. Carry your bag in your hand or get a strap pad to save on wear and tear.

333.

Polycotton shirts or blouses are cheaper and longer lasting than pure cotton, and require less ironing.

334.

Wear old clothes round the house, especially if doing dirty jobs, or just when relaxing. No sense wearing out good stuff.

335.

Sew or glue 'kick tape' (reinforcement tape) on the inside of trouser hems, especially jeans, to prevent fraying.

336.

If cuffs are too far gone for repair, simply cut off the sleeves and hem them with stitches or Wundaweb to make a short sleeve shirt. Keep the offcuts for patching.

337.

Always use wooden shoe trees in your shoes when not wearing them. It keeps them looking good for much longer and helps absorb damp and odours.

338.

Patches on the knees of adult trousers look odd – but if knees are wearing thin, patch them on the inside with iron patches or scrap material to make them last longer.

339.

Extend the life of worn bedsheets by 'sides to middle'. Cut the worn sheet down the middle, turn the two pieces round and then sew them together so that the worn areas are on the edges rather than the middle.

340.

A couple of thick magazines rolled up tightly make inexpensive boot stretchers.

341.

To reuse a snapped shoelace, tie the ends together and relace so that the knot is inside the shoe and can't be seen.

342.

Need to patch a garment but don't have matching material? Simply cut off the material from part of the garment that can't be seen, such as a shirt tail or the lining inside a sleeve. Patch over that hole with scrap material and use the matching piece where it will be seen.

343.

Don't throw away old socks too holey to wear. Wear them over a good pair to keep your feet warmer in winter.

344.

1.5 litre full plastic water bottles make cheap stretchers for high boots. Insert with the top end downwards into the boot.

345.

If a pillowcase becomes worn thin, sew up the open end, then sew the whole case onto a piece of scrap material the same size, (eg, from an old sheet) leaving one side open, to make a 'new' pillowcase.

346.

A woman's jumper or tee shirt with small moth holes, cigarette burn holes, wear holes, etc, can be restored by sewing sequins over the holes.

347.

Use the small right hand pocket of your jeans to store keys, coins etc, this will save wear and tear on the other pocket linings.

348.

Save money on mechanical fabric fuzz removers. Just use the 'hook' side of a piece of Velcro and rub the fabric briskly.

349.

Use scrunched up newspaper to dry wet shoes or boots. Keep them in a warm room but never use artificial heat such as putting them on a radiator to dry, as it ruins the leather.

350.

Save money by not buying an evening dress shirt with studs. Button covers can be bought online and fitted over the buttons of a normal white shirt.

351.

A tiny amount of polish on a duster will produce a high shine if you polish (or 'bull') your shoes military style. Find out how to do it on Youtube.

352.

If a hat is too big, put strips of newspaper or tissue paper inside the inner band to make it fit better.

353.

If a hat is too small, it can sometimes be made larger by steaming it and gently stretching the brim.

354.

Ties with frayed ends can still be worn under a v neck pullover or waistcoat – nobody will see the worn part.

355.

Don't spend money on vests or undershirts for winter. Just wear summer tee shirts under your shirt.

356.

Men who require morning or evening dress for formal events should look at the ex-hire departments of the large formal wear hire firms. Good quality clothing can sometimes be bought at little more than the cost of hiring.

357.

To adjust the size of a shirt collar, simply remove the top button and replace it nearer to or further from the button hole as required. You can adjust by about ¼ of an inch this way.

358.

Need a new watch? Consider if you need one at all, if you carry a mobile phone. You'll save money on battery replacements as well as the initial cost.

Don't throw away a jumper or jacket with worn elbows. Use iron on patches for a quick and long lasting repair.

359.

Splits in rubber shoe soles can be mended easily. Simply heat an old knife over a flame then gently rub the blade into the crack. Remove the blade and press the edges of the crack together then rub over the top of the crack with the knife to seal it.

360.

If your armchair or sofa has worn out arms, cut material from an unseen area, such as the back of the chair or the underside of the seat cushion, and use this for covering the worn areas. Use scrap material to patch over the 'donor' area. Fabric glue is quick and easy for this.

361.

Cheap shoes are usually a false economy. A pair of good shoes if maintained well and repaired, will last many years.

362.

Socks with cotton towelling on the inside are more comfortable and hardwearing than thin wool or cotton socks but cost about the same.

363.

If you like pure cotton sheets, choose seersucker or other textured cotton. This usually doesn't require ironing.

364.

Buying short sleeved shirts for summer wear in temperate climates such as the UK is a waste of money. Rolling your sleeves up will be just as effective and will mean you don't need to have different shirts for winter and summer.

365.

Buy multipacks of socks of the same colour. When a sock becomes too holey to wear, you can still make a up a pair with one of the others. This works for ladies' stockings too.

366.

Shoes need time to dry out from perspiration; don't wear the same pair of shoes twice in a row. Two pairs of shoes alternated will usually last longer than one pair worn every day.

367.

If you have a small ladder in your tights, applying a little clear nail varnish will stop it spreading.

368.

Use Fraycheck, a paint-on fabric strengthener, on frayed collars or cuffs or trouser hems. This can extend the life of garments a long time.

369.

Revive an old worn blazer with contrast bias tape on the cuffs, pocket edges and collar edges for that old-school look. This works well on ladies' blazers and suit jackets.

370.

A product called Shoe Goo, which can be used for simple shoe repairs at home, will pay for itself many times over. It is also useful for all kinds of repairs to leather and rubber etc.

371.

Tweed or leather is the best material for winter coats and jackets; it will last indefinitely.

372.

Frayed cuffs on tweed jackets can be mended with bias tape; it's not usually worth paying a professional to do this but if you have a sewing machine, try it yourself.

373.

Shoes need mending? Don't go to the cobblers. DIY kits are available online.

374.

If you have a shirt with a collar that's too frayed to save or turn, remove it altogether and sew up, to make a 'grandad' shirt.

375.

Avoid coats and jackets in light colours which will require more frequent cleaning.

376.

White trainers that have become grey and discoloured can be restored to a new appearance by using a white leather preparation such as Cherry Blosson Sports Whitener.

377.

Avoid coats and jackets in expensive but delicate fabrics like cashmere which wear out quickly.

378.

Shirt sleeves too long? Save money on alterations with sleeve garters available online. These are elasticated metal bands that will hold your shirtsleeves at just the right length.

379.

If you have a hole in your sock, it's not usually worth the time to darn it. Just sew up the hole instead - gives a few months' more wear.

380.

White shirts for formal wear can last longer, as slight fraying is less visible than on coloured shirts.

381.

Shirt collars can be turned quite easily if they are the type that don't have pockets for stiffeners. Using a scalpel or sharp knife, unpick the seam that holds the collar to the shirt. Flip over, and remove any built in stiffeners. Iron out wrinkles well with a steam iron. Put back in place and secure with fabric glue or Wundaweb. A shirt can be made to last years more this way.

382.

If you buy a new watch, choose one with a metal band. These last longer than leather straps.

383.

Avoid cheap corduroy jeans. These tend to go threadbare very quickly, especially at the knees. Cheap denim is about the same price but much more hardwearing.

384.

To patch linings in pockets etc, simply cut a piece of scrap material and paste it on with copydex or fabric glue. Saves time and money.

385.

Easycare polycotton sheets usually cost less and last longer than pure cotton, and require much less ironing.

386.

A cost-free way to make a ring fit better: simply cut small thin slivers of clear plastic tape (sellotape) and wrap carefully round the ring so it is barely visible. Keep the tape side on the inside of your hand when wearing the ring.

387.

Buy neutral coloured baby clothes etc if you plan to have more children.

388.

Don't rush out to buy clothes if you're pregnant. You'll receive a lot as gifts anyway.

389.

Save money on school uniforms by finding out if your child's school holds second hand uniform sales. If they don't, (some schools discourage it due to agreements with local uniform suppliers, or simple snobbery) try setting up a Facebook group yourself for fellow parents. Articles of uniform can be placed for auction on Ebay and the group can be notified by Facebook. This works also for Scouts, Guides, choristers, army cadets etc.

390.

Old flannelette sheets, shirts or pyjamas make ideal cleaning cloths, especially for glassware and spectacles. Just cut out squares to size using pinking shears.

391.

When tights become too laddered to wear, cut off and keep the 'good' legs until you can make a new pair by sewing together or just wearing one on top of the other.

392.

Shirt collar too tight? Don't buy new shirts. Use button extenders, available cheaply online. They just hook over the existing button to give extra room.

393.

Reusable nappies (diapers) can be cheaper than disposables, but remember to factor in time and laundry costs.

394.

If the cuffs on a shirt are too far gone for turning, cut off the sleeves and hem at elbow height to make a short sleeve shirt.

395.

An old lightbulb can be used as a 'darning mushroom' for mending socks etc. Just hold the bulb in your hand and stretch the sock over it while mending.

396.

The ribbon from conference and trade show ID badges is sturdy and can be used as kick tape (hemming reinforcement tape) in trouser hems.

397.

Keep laddered tights for use as legwarmers under jeans in cold weather.

398.

Divers' watches are tough and longer lasting as they're less likely to be damaged if scuffed or dropped.

399.

Don't spend money on special thick thread for mending. To make strong repair thread for clothing, simply double a length of thread and sew normally.

400.

There's no need for men to pay for patent leather evening dress shoes. Ordinary black shoes can be 'bulled' military style for a patent leather look when the need arises.

401.

Less is more with shoe polish. Just pat the end of a shoe brush into the polish then dip in cold water, and work the brush into the leather in a circular motion. No need to waste polish by smearing a big amount on a cloth.

402.

Wax crayons can be used to cover scuffed areas on boots and shoes, especially heels. This lasts longer than polish.

403.

Save old clothing for patching. Remove buttons and zips for later use.

404.

A worn out or stained garment can be completely refreshed by dyeing it with a washing machine dye. Make sure you wash the machine through after use and be careful when washing the garment as dyes can sometimes run.

405.

If a shirt cuff or trouser hem is too worn for Fraycheck, just turn

it inwards by about 1/8-1/4 of an inch so that the frayed area does not show. Iron in place and then either stitch or use fabric glue.

Holidays/vacations, travel and motoring

406.

Camping is a great way to save money on holiday. Find cheap camping sites using websites like pitchup.com

407.

Bicycle panniers are inexpensive and can carry quite large amounts of shopping if you want to avoid using the car or don't have one. Choose the type with carrying handle, this can be lifted off and taken into the supermarket with you.

408.

Nightclubs in holiday resorts sometimes have free entry earlier in the evening, while prices rocket as the night goes on. Go early for nothing and pace yourself.

409

A Network Railcard, costing £30 will save you money on journeys in the south east of England. It's worth it if you make regular rail journeys outside the Greater London area.

410.

Instant shoe shine sponges can be used to restore the shine on exterior and interior black plastic car trims.

411.

If you're a frequent flyer, there's no need to pay extortionate prices for airport drinks. British airports will allow up to one litre of liquids to be taken through security if it is in bottles of no more than 100ml. A set of small bottles in a clear plastic bag is available online. Fill them with water or juice and they will pay for themselves after a couple of flights.

412.

If you don't have children of school age, avoid going on holiday during school holiday time.

413.

Using the manual shift on an automatic transmission car is said to save on fuel.

414.

Check to see if the city you are visiting has weekly or fortnightly season tickets for public transport. These can work out dramatically cheaper than buying single tickets for each journey. Bring a couple of passport photos with you just in case; you may need to sign up for some sort of photocard.

Sometimes this may only be available to city residents, but you might be able to get away with giving the address of your hotel or a friend.

415.

When approaching a steep hill in your car, accelerate beforehand to gain momentum, this should use less fuel than straining the engine once on the hill.

416.

Worn out car seats? Stretch covers are available cheaply online or from car superstores.

417.

Find out if your workplace has a car pool system to save on commuting costs. If there isn't one, why not start one?

418.

When approaching a red traffic light from a distance, slow down well in advance rather than rushing. Hopefully it will turn green and you can continue without a stop/start, which wastes fuel.

419.

British citizens should always make sure they have an EHIC card when travelling to European Union countries. This is free of charge and provides reciprocal health care cover.

420.

When booking train tickets, check to see if it is cheaper to break your journey into two or three sections rather than one ticket for the entire journey.

421.

If breakfast is included in the price at your hotel, fill up on a Full English and you often won't need to buy lunch. Then have a picnic in your hotel room for the evening meal.

422.

Don't book excursions and trips with your hotel rep before shopping around first. These can often be arranged more cheaply with firms outside the hotel.

423.

Check carefully when booking budget flights. Very cheap flights sometimes land in airports a long way from your actual destination, or at a time when public transport is not running, which means you have to pay extra for taxis or hotels.

424.

A bicycle with hub gears will require less costly maintenance over its life than a derailleur system.

425.

When checking flight prices online, cancel cookies, delete history etc when surfing. It is said that some sites can detect your usage and will increase prices accordingly.

426.

To save money on entrance fees to cathedrals, attend one of the daily services instead, which are always free. Although you can't walk around, you will be able to admire the building from your pew, listen to the choir, and only pay what you put in the collection plate. Check first if the services take place in the main cathedral or a side chapel.

427.

Some credit card companies offer travel insurance free with their cards; it is worth opening an account if you are a regular traveller – but remember, always pay your balance in full at the end of the month!

428.

If you park regularly in the same place, check parking space rental websites. These are garages or driveways rented out by residents. It can be cheaper than paying for long term parking in stations, car parks etc.

429.

Get quotes from three garages before agreeing to repair work on your car.

430.

Buy a folding bike; these can be bought quite cheaply on Ebay. When driving to somewhere with expensive parking, keep the bike in your car boot to enable you to park somewhere further away which has free parking.

431.

Weigh up the advantages of distance versus cost on holiday. For example, a holiday in your own country doesn't involve much travel, but costs can be high (especially if you live in the UK). Travel abroad to Europe is cheap, but costs can be equally high in some places when you get there. Travel to places further afield, such as Thailand, costs much more, but prices of food and accommodations are radically cheaper once you get there.

432.

Take your own sun umbrella, mats etc to the beach. Loungers usually cost money and it all adds up over the course of a week or two.

433.

Try walking to work to save commuting costs. Three miles each way is realistic for most people and can be done in about an hour. You'll also dramatically improve your health.

Special travel clothes such as those made by Tilley are available which will dry quickly overnight. Although these cost money upfront, if you cut your clothing down when travelling you will save huge amounts by only having to have cabin luggage on flights.

434.

Note the number of your bicycle frame, it will be on the underside where the pedals meet the frame. If your bicycle is stolen and later recovered by the police it is the only sure way to identify it.

435.

If you're a regular cyclist, change your bicycle tyres to Schwalbe Marathon puncture proof tyres. These are more expensive initially but you will save a huge amount of time and money in the long run.

436.

Coach travel can be a very inexpensive way to explore continental Europe. Eurolines coaches offer 15 or 30 day passes which give huge discounts if you are travelling a lot.

437.

Accelerate gradually; avoid revving the engine. This saves fuel.

438.

If you eat out, choose lunch instead of dinner for your main meal. This is usually cheaper.

439.

If you don't mind sharing a room, youth hostels can be a very cheap way of staying in new places in the UK and abroad. There is usually no membership charge or upper age limit.

440.

Some large bookstores will allow you to sit and browse indefinitely with no obligation to purchase; check out tourist guides while travelling.

441.

Moneysaving Expert has a list of all free museums and art galleries in the UK here: http://www.moneysavingexpert.com/deals/free-museums-and-art-galleries

442.

If you take sandwiches with you on a city tour you can eat in parks etc during good weather. In winter or if the weather's bad it can be more difficult. One solution is to eat on the concourse of a railway station or on a bench in a shopping mall; nobody is likely to object.

443.

Check out the transport arrangements from airports to city centres before you arrive. In the confusion of the airport terminal it's easy to be hustled by overpriced taxi drivers or worse, con artists. There is nearly always a cheaper public transport alternative to taxis at airports.

444.

A narrow boat holiday can be very cheap, as it combines transport and accommodation in one, but only if you have enough people to share the cost. This is best for groups of friends. Boating holidays for less than four people can be prohibitively expensive.

445.

When visiting a foreign city, check its public transport website beforehand. (They usually have English translations). This will give you valuable information on moneysaving deals without the hassle of having to find out when you arrive. There are often reciprocal arrangements for free travel for senior citizens from other European countries.

446.

If you can't finish your meal in a restaurant, ask for a 'doggy bag' to take home your leftovers for later. UK restaurants can sometimes be a bit snooty about this but it's normal practice in many countries including the USA.

447.

Use public loos whenever possible on boating holidays;

this will save pump out costs for the on-board lavatory.

448.

Tailor made clothing can be very cheap in the Far East, especially in Hong Kong and Thailand. Be wary of scams however – check tourist forums before going and always use your credit card for protection.

449.

Shop around for meal deals. Wetherspoon's pubs are usually the cheapest places to eat in the UK for breakfast, lunch or dinner, and have free wi-fi also.

450.

Keep your money safe on holiday with a travel wallet worn under clothing. These can be bought cheaply online, or you can make one yourself quite easily with scrap cloth if you're good with sewing. Keep a 'decoy' wallet or purse in your pocket or bag also, with a few low denomination notes and unwanted cards. Foreign pickpockets often target tourists on public transport etc.

451.

If you have a smart phone, check if airlines, bus companies, hotels etc will accept an on-screen version of your ticket instead of a printed one. This saves on printing and paper costs.

452.

Don't fill the petrol tank to the top. Fuel creates extra weight, so keeping the tank half full will use less fuel.

453.

An ISIC (International Student Identity Card) offers discounts for full time students worldwide.

454.

Turn your engine off at traffic lights; some modern cars even do this automatically as a fuel economy feature.

455.

Make friends with the barmen or waiters in your hotel or local bar in holiday resorts. You will often get given bigger portions, free shots, etc; in some countries drinks measures are not regulated so a happy barman will give you a bigger drink. A tip at the end of your holiday would be a polite gesture in return.

456.

If you smoke or drink, remember to take advantage of duty free allowances or cheaper alcohol and tobacco, but check customs regulations carefully. British smokers can save huge amounts by a single trip to France.

457.

If you are staying at an airport hotel, check to see if there is a free shuttle bus from the airport. Many hotels offer this service at no extra charge.

458.

Check entry tariffs at museums, galleries etc carefully; sometimes there will be free entry at certain times or on certain days.

459.

A dark coloured car will require less washing and doesn't show scuffs and corrosion spots as much as one in a light colour.

460.

Work out the cost per mile for petrol in your car. Keep a jar in the car and 'pay' to use it each time you drive. Use the cash each time you fill up the tank. This ensures you always have petrol money and don't take unnecessary journeys.

461.

Travel and accommodation costs make up a large part of holiday expenses, so why not try a 'holiday at home.' Take a week or two off work but stay at home; spend the days out at local places of interest and treat yourself to restaurant meals in the evening.

462.

Take budget flights midweek if possible. Flights are usually cheapest on Tuesdays and Wednesdays.

463.

If you're going out drinking, have supper first. You'll feel less like drinking lots of expensive beer.

464.

Holidays in winter are usually much cheaper than in summer. Places like the Canary Islands, north Africa and southern Europe often have good weather during the winter months when flights and hotels are dramatically cheaper.

465.

Cheap and easy car wash: when it's about to rain, take a spray bottle with some liquid soap in and spritz it all over the car; then sit back and let the rain rinse it off.

466.

Beware of any people who offer to be your guide etc at tourist hotspots. They are usually after money and can become quite unpleasant if you don't pay them after using their 'services'. If in doubt, ask for official identification.

467.

A 'penny stove' which uses methylated spirits is much cheaper than using a calor gas stove when camping. They are available cheaply online, sometimes made from recycled aluminium drink cans.

468.

If you only need a flight, sometimes a package deal including a hotel can work out cheaper than a regular scheduled flight ticket.

469.

When travelling outside Europe, remember to check if visas or inoculations are required for your destination. This can significantly add to the cost of a bargain holiday, especially for a whole family. The Foreign Office website has details of requirements.

470.

Steer clear of tourist traps wherever possible, these are designed to part you from your cash as quickly as possible. Try taking a local bus and going somewhere off the tourist trail – you may be pleasantly surprised.

471.

Save money on expensive bicycle chain cleaning gadgets. Simply fix two old toothbrushes together with gaffer tape over your bicycle chain, spray degreasant on the chain and run it round a few times.

472.

If you have a flight transfer which involves a few hours wait in an airport, it's worth sleeping in the terminal instead of getting a hotel. Many airports won't like you bedding down in a sleeping bag on the floor but if you stretch out on a bench somewhere discrete you may get away with it. Use an eye mask to block out bright light.

473.

Always use the handbrake (emergency brake) on hill starts. Using the clutch as a hill brake wears it out more quickly.

474.

Keep an eye out for pumice stone on the beach. This is common on volcanic beaches such as those in the Canary Islands, Greece and Italy. It is useful for rubbing off hard skin and cleaning tough stains off hands. A few stones will last a lifetime.

475.

Consider changing your working hours/travelling times to avoid stop/start traffic in busy periods.

476.

Stay with friends or relations on holiday to save money – but remember, you're duty bound to reciprocate.

477.

If you have a few hours to kill when travelling, shopping malls are good places to go where you can keep warm (or cool) and read a book on a bench in relative comfort and safety, and they also have washing facilities. But don't buy anything, or you won't have saved money!

478.

Commercial arts and crafts galleries can be very interesting to visit and don't need to cost you anything. If there is any pressure on you to buy, just politely excuse yourself and leave.

479.

Want a free tent? Some festival-goers ditch their camping equipment before going home; so hang around at the end of a concert and ask politely if you see anything left behind.

480.

Instead of expensive hand sanitizers, use vinegar from a small spray bottle when travelling. The smell will quickly disappear but you can add essential oils just in case.

481.

Alterations are much quicker and cheaper in developing countries. If buying clothes abroad, get them altered before you leave for home.

482.

Green Line bus services run from central London to airports and are cheaper than rail or taxis. They are also free for senior citizen pass holders.

483.

Car hire firms recommended by hotels or based in hotels are

often overpriced. Shop around the resort for a deal.

484.

The further they are from the terminal, the cheaper the airport hotels are, so shop around for bargains. As mentioned, many offer free shuttle services so it won't cost you anything more than a few extra minutes of your time to get there.

485.

If on a boating holiday, use British Waterways moorings, which are usually free.

486.

The Interrail pass (or Eurail pass for non-EU residents) offers large discounts on rail travel on the continent. Prices are much lower if you only want to explore one country, and people under 26 get further discounts.

487.

Have your car MOT done at a council test centre. They do not undertake repairs so have no vested interest in failing you.

488.

Cardboard covered with tinfoil makes a cheap sunblind for a parked car.

489.

Fill up your car with petrol early in the morning. Fuel becomes less dense as the day warms up and you get fractionally less for your money.

490.

Beware of attempts by museums and galleries to make you think that you have to pay for entry, when you don't. Signs will sometimes be worded in such a way to fool, or embarrass you, into paying 'suggested donations' when you don't actually have to.

491.

Dull tasting tobacco can be improved by spritzing with a little brandy or whisky and leaving a few days in the tin or pouch.

492.

Use park and ride facilities when driving to large towns.

493.

Be careful about hotels that include breakfast. Check if it is full English or just a continental breakfast; often the extra cost is not worth it as breakfast can be bought more cheaply in cafes.

494.

Drive in the highest gear possible without straining the engine. This saves fuel.

495.

Avoid the minimarkets and small supermarkets in holiday resorts close to hotels, these are often very overpriced. The shops that the local use will usually be quite nearby and much cheaper.

496.

Use airbnb.com or couch surfing websites to save money on hotels.

497.

Walk or cycle whenever you can, especially if it means you save on bus fares.

498.

If you have a caravan, join the Caravan Club. This gives access to many cheap camping sites.

499.

When driving, wear light, thin soled shoes rather than heavy boots or shoes. This will enable you to drive more sensitively and thus save fuel.

500.

Coach travel can be much cheaper than trains, especially if you book in advance with companies like Megabus. The journey may take a little longer but coaches are usually comfortable and equipped with wi-fi and toilet facilities.

501.

All inclusive deals are often big money savers for families, as long as you don't mind eating and drinking in the same hotel every day.

502.

Special travel coats are available, such as those made by Rufus Roo. These have huge pockets but are classified as clothing by budget airlines, enabling you to take more on board the plane and thus save money on luggage costs. Once you get your seat, just take the coat off and put it in the luggage rack.

503.

Padded cycling shorts are usually a waste of money unless you are a competitive cyclist For normal touring, two pairs of ordinary underpants worn under shorts or trousers will cut down on chafing.

504.

Don't throw out a suitcase if the wheels have broken. The wheels are usually the first thing to break but the case can last for many more years. Instead, buy a folding luggage trolley to strap your case to. This also works well for older or vintage suitcases that don't have wheels. It can also be used by the elderly or infirm to carry small loads around the house .

505.

Avoid expensive parking charges at the station – buy a cheap bicycle and ride there instead.

506.

Remove any unnecessary weight from the car when not in use – roofrack, snow shovel in summer, etc.

507.

If you need travel vaccinations, check with your NHS doctor's surgery first, as this can often be cheaper than using private travel clinics.

508.

Don't throw away a bicycle saddle if it's worn out – use a gel saddle cover available online or from bike shops. This will be cheaper than a new saddle and more comfortable.

509.

Avoid complicated parking manoeuvres, these waste fuel.

510.

Use AC in the car as little as possible - in the UK it's hardly ever needed.

511.

If you have leftover foreign currency at the end of your holiday, try offering it to fellow tourists (discretely) in your hotel, at a favourable rate. This will save both of you money.

512.

Use a petrol cashback credit card – but be sure to pay the balance off in full each month.

513.

Take a large plastic water barrel or water carrying pouch when camping. Fill up with very hot water from the showers and use to keep you warm in your sleeping bag at night. Use for a quick wash or boil up for cooking in the morning.

514.

If you have a Transport for London season ticket, always check when booking if it will get you any discounts on rail journeys to destinations outside London.

515.

Don't spend money on car air fresheners. A few drops of essential oil on cotton wool or folded tissue paper will work just as well.

516.

Ask at carpet shops if they have any unwanted sample books. These have squares of carpet about 12"x12" which are ideal for using as small mats such as in car seatwells to save on carpet wear.

517.

Watch out for tourist money-grabbing scams, especially in developing countries. Check tourist forums and websites for the country before you visit to get the unofficial lowdown- often these scams won't be mentioned on official websites in order not to deter tourists.

518.

Visiting historic houses, palaces etc can be costly. An alternative is to just visit the gardens, which are cheaper or sometimes free.

519.

Public lavatories abroad often have to be paid for. Most museums and galleries though usually won't charge, so if entry is free anyway, just drop in and use the facilities.

520.

If public transport in your holiday city is cheap and reliable, consider staying in a hotel or apartment farther out of the city centre and travelling in each day. Prices will often be much lower.

521.

Check comparison sites for the best car insurance deals.

522.

A cycling and wild camping holiday is probably about the cheapest possible holiday you can take.

523.

To save on expensive hotel laundries or launderettes when travelling, just wash items in your hotel sink each night. Take a length of string to make a clothesline.

524.

If you have a three speed bicycle, leave the gear lever in third when not riding. This prevents strain on the cable and will lengthen its life.

525.

Don't pay for loos in railway stations. Try to hang on until you get on the train where the loos are free.

526.

Keep car tyre pressure correct to reduce fuel use.

527.

When travelling by train on the continent consider getting a couchette or sleeper car; in some cases it could prove cheaper than a night in a hotel.

528.

Use a prepaid currency card when abroad, this is usually much cheaper than using bureaux de change.

529.

For a cheap night out, buy some drinks from the supermarket and enjoy on your hotel terrace; then hit the town for just one or two drinks.

530.

Avoid excess luggage charges at the airport by weighing your luggage carefully at home before leaving. There's no need to buy a special scale, just stand on an ordinary bathroom scale while holding the luggage, then deduct your body weight from the total. Remember to allow for any presents or souvenirs you're planning on buying when away.

531.

Avoid air ticket agencies. These often practice 'bait and switch' by luring you into booking cheap deals, which then mysteriously vanish. Buying direct from the airline's website is usually the cheapest and safest way.

532.

As a general rule, cafes and bars get less expensive the further away they are from the centre of holiday resorts; you can often save money simply walking half a mile or so along the beach.

533.

When driving, slow naturally where possible, by stepping off the gas, rather than braking (obviously not in emergencies!)

534.

Use lift sharing services such as liftshare.com to save money on transport.

535.

Use a fuel comparison site like petrolprices.com to check the best price on fuel in your area

536.

Take a folding bicycle when on boating holidays. This will enable you to use free mooring spots away from the very crowded paid-for moorings close to popular locations.

537.

Learn to service your own bike; this will save lots of money. Most things can be done pretty easily once you know how, and there are lots of Youtube tutorials to help. If you are taking something apart and are not sure how to fix it, take pictures of each step using your phone or digital camera.

538.

Budget airlines such as Easyjet sometimes have shuttle bus services from city centres to airports that are much cheaper than trains or taxis. Check when booking.

539.

For more than one or two people, renting a city centre apartment will nearly always work out cheaper than using a hotel, and will have cooking facilities to help you save even more money.

540.

Working holidays for charities and overseas aid agencies can sometimes include free or subsidised food and accommodation.

541.

Camping with a car? Special car tents are available which attach on to the back or side of your car, dramatically increasing the space available for camping.

542.

Vinegar sprayed on the car windscreen is said to prevent frost forming. It's certainly cheaper than commercial sprays for the same purpose.

543.

The end of a long train journey is the time to pick up free newspapers and magazines – keep an eye out for discarded copies. If you're about to start your journey from the terminus, have a quick look through the windows of nearby trains that have just arrived in order to get some free reading matter for your journey.

544.

Get rid of your car altogether – try a car club if there is one in your area.

545.

Sunglasses can get scratched or damaged easily on holiday. Always carry them in a case to help them last longer.

546.

Save money on meals in hotels by using packet soups and other dried foods such as noodles; heat them up using the kettle or buy a heating element or travel kettle.

547.

Department stores and shopping malls usually have free lavatories, but these can be quite well hidden. In department stores they are usually on the top floor at the back, in the hope that you'll see something you want to buy before you get there!

548.

An Annual Gold Card holder can enable another person to buy a Network Railcard for just £1. If you work in London, ask around friends or colleagues to see if anyone is willing to offer it to you.

549.

Try wild camping where allowed. For example, it's legal in most parts of Scotland. This saves on camp site costs.

550.

Keep to 56mph on the motorway. This is said to be the optimum speed for fuel economy on most vehicles.

551.

If you have a pensioner's bus pass and time is not an issue, you can travel pretty much anywhere in the UK free of charge. Plan your route carefully online to connect local services, and avoid paying anything even for long distance travel.

Entertainment and leisure

552.

Alcohol is often the most expense part of a meal out. Check if there are restaurants in your area without a drinks licence, which allow you to bring your own – as long as they do not charge a fee (called 'corkage').

553.

At Christmas or birthdays, wrapping paper can be reused. Simply cut off any sections with sellotape attached then use a warm iron to smooth out any wrinkles. If you don't want to look 'cheap' in front of others, just gather up the paper and say 'I'll get this out of the way' then put it in another room for later.

554.

Instead of buying books, swap them using an online service such as readitswapit.co.uk

555.

Save money on TV guides by using the guide on your digibox instead.

556.

Don't waste money on expensive laptop/notebook

sleeves. A large bubble wrap envelope works just as well.

557.

Modern wine glasses tend to be large, which can make you drink more. Use old fashioned smaller glasses instead to save money. These are often available in charity shops, and can sometimes be stronger than modern glasses as well.

558.

Make a cheap picnic hamper look better by replacing the plastic plates and glassware for real china and glass from charity shops. A gingham table cloth keeps everything wrapped up nicely and completes the traditional look.

559.

Second hand copies of most books are available on Amazon, from as little as a penny plus postage.

560.

Drink shandy (half beer, half lemonade) every other pint in the pub.

561.

Save money on birthday and Christmas cards by reusing old ones. Cut the card in half and keep the back page for scrap, scribble pads etc. Then stick the front to a slightly larger, dark coloured piece of textured, folded card. Use gold or silver pens to write the inscription.

562.

A good quality artificial Christmas tree can look as good as a real one and will last indefinitely, saving you money year after year. Also, it won't shed needles on the carpet.

563.

Don't spend money on expensive Ebook covers. You can make your own easily from unwanted second hand hardback books. Youtube videos will show you how.

564.

Theatre visits can be expensive – why not try your local amateur theatre group or performing arts college; tickets are much cheaper than the professional theatre.

565.

Give up the TV licence and use internet catch-up services instead. To comply with the law in the UK you will need to get rid of your television set.

566.

One or one and a half litre water bottles make free weights for home work outs. Use water bottles with a narrow middle for easier grip.

567.

Modelling clay (playdough/plasticine type) for children can be made cheaply at home. Mix 1 cup of flour, 1 tsp vegetable oil, 1/4 cup salt and 1/3 cup of water and knead until smooth. Add food colourings if desired.

568.

Books will be less likely to have faded covers and browned pages if they are kept in a bookcase with glass doors out of direct sunlight. They will then keep better for resale.

569.

Start a book swap at work; many people buy new books and get rid of them quite soon after reading.

570.

Essential foraging/blackberrying kit: old, thornproof and waterproof clothes; a walking stick or grabbing handle for pulling branches closer; wellingtons or boots for muddy, thorny undergrowth; stout gardening gloves, a large rucksack or sidepack, and plenty of plastic bags and boxes.

571.

Some cathedrals and churches hold regular free organ recitals. Enjoy top quality classical music in historic surroundings free of charge.

572.

Make homemade personalised greetings cards on your computer. Use images of films, pop stars etc that the person likes. You can include 'in' jokes or jokes from humour websites. Use a good quality stiff paper to print out, or use ordinary paper and glue to card. There are lots of online tutorials to help.

573.

Make rolling tobacco go further by adding herbal smoking mixture, available online or from health food shops. Warning – don't mix more than about three quarters tobacco to one quarter herbs, or you might get some funny looks when people smell it!

574.

In the pub, always check draught beer to make sure you've been given full measure. Sometimes inexperienced bar staff give you a lot of foam instead of beer at the top.

575.

If you're anxious about serving cheap spirits to guests, put them into glass decanters available cheaply from pound shops, charity shops etc.

576.

If you smoke and can't or don't want to give up, change to roll your own cigarettes Handrolling machines are cheap and easy to use to make a professional looking cigarette. Keep them in a cigarette case (available cheaply online) for a stylish look.

577.

If you have the tobacco habit and can't give up, changing to e-cigarettes , a pipe, or even snuff (powdered tobacco), will also save lots of money.

578.

Get children to help in the garden or on foraging trips. It's fun and educational – and saves you work!

579.

Slip-on plastic book covers for paperbacks are cheap and easy to use. They will keep your books in better condition should you wish to sell them later via Amazon or car boot sales etc.

580.

End of line rolls of wallpaper can be bought very cheaply from DIY shops and make great wrapping paper for gifts or for lining drawers.

581.

Try a 'fast' with an activity which costs money, such as smoking, eating chocolates or drinking alcohol, during Lent. This will save money but won't look cheap.

582.

If you can't find a particular book in your public library, ask if it can be ordered or borrowed through the Inter-Library Loans service. There may be a small charge.

583.

Tobacco stays fresh longer if you put a piece of clean damp tissue paper in the tin or pouch. Don't use a piece of apple as some recommend, as this can cause mould.

584.

If you are buying wrapping paper, choose a neutral design

that can be used for both Christmas and birthday gifts.

585.

To revitalise stale rolling tobacco, spritz it with water from a spray bottle until it is slightly damp, then seal up and leave for a couple of days.

586.

Guitar plectrums can be made cheaply by cutting out squares from old credit cards.

587.

Old comics can be used as colourful wrapping paper for children's presents.

588.

To make ribbons for gift wrapping, cut strips from old clothes or sheets using pinking shears. This works best with colourful or patterned satin materials such as linings.

589.

Greetings cards are much cheaper from market stalls than shops.

590.

Instead of giving cut flowers as a present to a loved one in your family, give a flowering pot plant instead. This can provide years of pleasure instead of just the few days that cut flowers will last for.

591.

Make Christmas gift tags by cutting up old Christmas cards into smaller pieces, and folding them.

592.

Take sandwiches to work or whenever you need to eat outside your home.

593.

Free books are easily available to read on Kindle or smart phones (in PDF format); check out Project Gutenberg or the Internet Archive.

594.

Choose your hobbies carefully. There are four kinds of hobbies: 1: those that cost money, 2: those that don't cost anything, 3: those that save you money, and 4: those that make you money. Obviously you should try to have hobbies in categories 2-4!

595.

Cancel any magazine or newspaper subscriptions. You can have 'library night' or get the information free online.

596.

If you roll your own cigarettes, save on filters by substituting a small rolled up piece of paper or card. This means you use less tobacco. It will also have a slight filtering effect, although not as much as a proper filter tip.

597.

Buy Christmas decorations, wrapping paper, non-perishable gifts etc immediately after Christmas when prices are much cheaper.

598.

Unwanted CDs can be used as coasters.

599.

Worn out mens' shirts can be reused as painting or cooking smocks for children, if worn back to front.

600.

Elasticated hotel shower caps make great covers for plates and bowls of food in the fridge.

Cleaning and laundry

601.

'Iron a lot while the iron's hot'. Heating an iron for one or two items wastes energy.

602.

A bowl of vinegar in a room will absorb bad smells such as stale tobacco smoke. Spritzing the air with vinegar from a spray bottle will also help.

603.

Steam cleaning and 'sponge and press' can save huge amounts on dry cleaning. A domestic steamer can be used to freshen up clothes. To give a deeper clean, sponge down garments with a large clean sponge until they are damp, then press with a hot iron over a clean cloth. The dirt rises out in the steam on the same principle as a Turkish bath.

604.

Save the soapy water that collects in the bottom of the soap dish in a sealed jar or bottle, this can then be used as a liquid cleaner for worktops, bicycles etc.

605.

If you have a jacket with smelly armpits and all else has failed, try squeezing a solution of Woolite wool cleaner and cold water through the affected area with a clean sponge. Leave on for a few hours to soak in then squeeze cold water through to rinse. This should only be done as a last resort as it could shrink or damage the fabric and interlinings.

606.

Cheap cola can be used to clean brass items. Simply soak them until clean.

607.

Turn clothes inside out when washing (especially dark clothes) and make sure all zips, buttons etc are done up; this reduces wear on the clothes and the machine drum.

608.

Make new soap from old; when scraps become too small to use keep them in an airtight container. When you have enough to make a new bar, boil them gently in a pan with a little water then pour into a container such as an old yoghurt pot or cream cheese tub to set into a new bar.

609.

Don't use the whole of a metal scouring pad; break off only as much as you need for the job in hand. This way you don't have to leave a damp pad to rust away.

610.

A paste made from salt and olive oil is said to remove heat rings from furniture. Leave for an hour then wipe off.

611.

Store brooms with the brush end off the floor to extend their life.

612.

If you have a stained white garment, if all else fails try dabbing neat bleach on to the spot with a cotton wool bud, or the point of a needle for small spots.

613.

Cheap silver cleaner: mix half a cup of vinegar and two tablespoons of bicarbonate of soda. Leave silver to soak for three hours, then rinse and wipe off.

614.

Save time and energy costs by folding sheets in half and ironing on one side only.

615.

Top up thick bleach bottles with water, it works just as well and goes further.

616.

Keep old socks for cleaning mitts. They are great for fiddly jobs like cleaning venetian blinds or filthy work like degreasing a bicycle chain.

617.

Don't buy 'drawer fresheners'; storing your soap bars in your chest of drawers does the job just as well.

618.

To increase drying space on washing lines, hook a length of plastic garden chain over the line. Shirts on hangers can then be hooked onto the chain.

619.

If your steam iron doesn't give off steam but still heats, don't throw it out. Simply fill a spray bottle with water and spray items before ironing.

620.

Clean out clothes cupboards at least twice a year and vacuum thoroughly to prevent moths. Shake out clothes and check for holes while you do it.

621.

Use a squeezed lemon to clean mirrors, chrome surfaces etc; just rub on then wipe off with a clean cloth.

622.

Grouting can be cleaned with equal parts Epsom Salts and liquid soap.

623.

Most paper vacuum cleaner bags can be re-used several times. Remove carefully and empty. Mend with masking tape if they get ripped (wipe off surface dust with a cloth first).

624.

Don't waste money on bleach etc to sterilise cleaning cloths. Just put in a bowl of water in the microwave and heat until they're almost boiling.

625.

A plastic washing up bowl in the sink will require less hot water than filling the entire sink, and is more hygienic if you also use the sink for dirty jobs such as cleaning paint brushes etc. It also makes it easier to carry the rinse water out to pour into your garden watering can.

626.

Tumble dryers are expensive and can damage clothes. Hang clothes out to dry on the line or on an airer indoors instead.

627.

Lemon juice can be used to remove stains from clothing. Work in well then wash as normal.

628.

Don't use a scrubbing brush to work soap or pre-stain treatments into shirt collars before washing them. This wears them out quickly. Just rub the soap straight on.

629.

Vinegar can be used in place of fabric conditioner, especially in hard water areas.

630.

Polish windows and glass with half water, half vinegar from a spray bottle.

631.

For cheap silver polish, make a paste of equal parts water and sodium bicarbonate. Brush or rub on then rinse and buff dry.

632.

A steam cleaner is inexpensive and saves time and money on jobs like degreasing ovens, cleaning carpets, curtains and soft furnishings, and can be used to clean dry-clean only clothing.

633.

A little lemon juice in the washing up water will cut the grease and make the washing up liquid go further.

634.

Try washing more items at 30c or even cold; most things (except towels and sheets) will be just as clean.

635.

Lemon juice can be used as an insect repellent. Squirt it around any areas of the house affected.

636.

Don't spend money on ironing board covers. An old bedsheet folded and secured tightly with safety pins works just as well.

637.

To remove tenacious black mould from grout, windowsills etc, soak toilet paper or kitchen roll in bleach and press it well into the mouldy area. Leave overnight to soak then remove the paper and rinse off.

638.

J-cloths can be laundered in the washing machine for re-use.

639.

Cut up old tee shirts, pants etc for cleaning cloths, oily rags etc. Use pinking shears to ensure the edges don't run.

640.

A damp sponge dipped in wood ash can be used to clean sooty stove doors.

641.

Used coffee grounds can be used to clean and deodorise smelly work surfaces, fridges, chopping boards etc. Simply rub in well with a sponge then rinse off.

642.

Old fashioned scouring powder (Vim, Ajax etc) goes much further than cream cleaners for the kitchen and bathroom.

643.

Dry rubber gloves gently after use and hang up separately. If stored close together they can stick, causing damage to the rubber.

644.

A smelly leather watchstrap can be deodorised by rubbing in bicarbonate of soda after you take it off at night.

645.

Use less washing powder. Half the recommended amount usually works just as well and is better for your machine.

646.

No need to spend money on air freshener for loos. Just open the window to air the room. If there's no window, a lit match or cigarette lighter waved around for a few seconds is said to clear most smells.

647.

Dry clean only clothing with persistently smelly underarm areas can be deodorised by making a paste of half water, half sodium bicarbonate. Work into the lining with an old brush and leave overnight, then dust off. Do a spot check first.

648.

A small amount of Vaseline on a duster can be used as a cheaper alternative to furniture polish.

649.

Ziploc bags can be washed and reused for food storage; this includes the bags that coffee etc come in.

650.

To make a cheap version of 'Febreze' fabric spray: mix one part cheap vodka to four parts water with optional essential oils, and use in a spray bottle.

651.

If your washing up brush or mop has worn out, wrap a couple of old plastic orange netting bags around the head and tie securely to make a 'new' brush.

652.

Costly pre-wash stain treatments usually aren't necessary. An ordinary bar of soap rubbed on the problem area before washing will remove most stains. This works well for 'ring around the collar'.

653.

To reinforce value black bin liners (which are prone to splitting) put a couple of sheets of newspaper in the bottom of the bag before using. This will strengthen the bag by distributing weight better, and will act as a barrier if the bag splits on the underside.

654.

Ironing uses energy and causes extra wear on clothes. Many clothes don't really need ironing and can just be smoothed, folded and put away; piles of clothing will naturally press themselves under their own weight.

655.

Cut down on soap powder in your washing machine. Manufacturer's recommended amounts are usually too much. It's better for your machine as well.

656.

Spray vinegar on aluminium and chrome fittings then buff off for a high shine.

657.

Save power when ironing; use the hot setting first on cottons, linens etc then switch off to iron manmade fabrics as the iron cools down.

658.

If one rubber glove in a pair is no good, keep the good one. The next time a rubber glove breaks you can use the old one to make up a new pair. If you have two left or two right gloves, simply turn one inside out to make up a new pair.

659.

Blocked showerhead? Soak it overnight in vinegar to destroy the limescale. If you can't remove the head, simply tie a plastic bag full of vinegar around it.

660.

Spray vinegar in areas of ant infestation, it acts as a repellent.

661.

Save money on oven cleaners. Wipe with a damp cloth and sprinkle on sodium bicarbonate. Leave overnight then rinse off.

662.

If an item of clothing isn't smelly and doesn't show any dirt, consider if it really needs to go in the wash.

663.

Banana skin (inside) can be used to shine the leaves of household plants.

664.

Your dishwasher can be used to clean dishcloths etc. This is a good way of using up space if you need to wash some dishes but don't have enough to fill the machine.

665.

Soda crystals are cheap and will soften your washing water, meaning less soap is needed. They are also useful for soaking dirty clothing before washing or general cleaning.

666.

Save leaky rubber gloves for dirty but 'dry' jobs around the house or garden.

667.

If a stain can't be removed from fabric, try using fabric paints to cover it. This works well with patterned items like tweed. You can buy small pots of matt enamel paints from model shops to make an exact colour match.

668.

Avoid clothes brushes made from a roll of sticky paper; this can build up small deposits of glue on the fabric.

669.

Use balls of wet newspaper to clean and polish windows, it gives a better shine than most spray-on products.

670.

Newspaper can be used to deodorise musty smelling cases, drawers etc. Scrunch up clean newspaper and stuff the item; leave overnight.

671.

Don't waste money on expensive shoe deodorisers. A sprinkling of sodium bicarbonate at night and shaken out in the morning will get rid of most smells. Alternatively try spritzing them inside with white vinegar.

672.

A plunger is a must-have. It will clear most sink blockages and can save a fortune in plumber's charges.

673.

You don't need to buy a special broom to clean laminate

flooring. An ordinary dry mop spritzed with white vinegar will give a good shine.

674.

Soaking laundry overnight before washday requires you to use less washing powder.

675.

Save energy by shaking out and smoothing items before hanging them on the line to dry, they will require less ironing or none at all.

676.

Hang up mops to dry; leaving them on the floor when damp makes them rot more easily.

677.

Always wear an apron in the kitchen and roll your sleeves up – just a few grease spots can ruin good clothing.

678.

White bread can be used to clean walls. Simply roll into a ball and use it on stains as you would a rubber/eraser.

679.

Shirt cuffs will last longer if you iron them flat, rather than folded.

The fold creates a point which frays more quickly.

680.

Save energy and money on washing woollen jumpers by simply pressing them with a damp cloth on the ironing board. This will clean and refresh them and won't risk shrinkage.

681.

Give longer life to your washing machine by occasionally running it empty using soda crystals instead of powder.

682.

Always use a clothes brush on non-washable items such as coats and jackets; it keeps them clean and less at risk from moths.

683.

When hanging clothes outside to dry, keep them out of direct sunlight. Clothes can be ruined by fading in a short time.

684.

Shiny suit elbows can be made to look new again by rubbing very gently with a high grade sandpaper.

685.

Run your washing machine on the economy/cold setting. This will work well for most clothes, although sheets and towels should be washed in hot water.

686.

Get the last bits of polish from a shoe polish tin by using the clean end of a burnt matchstick.

687.

Air freshener and ironing sprays can be made for pennies. Simply fill a spray bottle with water and add some essential oils. These are available cheaply from pound shops, market stalls etc.

688.

Try cutting dishwasher tablets in half; often they will work just as well as a whole one.

689.

Keep old toothbrushes for cleaning jobs, they're particularly good for cleaning bicycle chains or getting into the welts and soles of dirty shoes.

690.

Don't buy any more expensive cleaning products. Nearly all household jobs can be done with detergent, lemon juice, soda crystals and vinegar.

691.

A lemon or lemon juice can be used to deodorise smelly chopping boards, fridges etc.

692.

Wash up the least soiled items first (glassware etc) so that you don't have to change the hot water too often.

693.

Press shirt collars and cuffs firmly when ironing rather than rubbing with iron, which wears them out more quickly.

694.

Free stain remover for grease spots: place some greaseproof paper over the stain then press with a hot iron. Also works for wax stains.

695.

A washing up mop with a built in liquid dispenser will save you a lot of money in washing up liquid.

696.

To give a splayed toothbrush a new lease of life for cleaning jobs, press the bristles overnight in a vice or doorjamb.

697.

Scrunch up the net bags that oranges come in and use them as pot scrubbers or even exfoliators in the bathroom.

698.

If your machine has a quick wash programme try this; it will get most clothes just as clean as on longer cycles.

699.

Cheap silver polish: to a saucepan of one litre of water, add one tablespoon of sodium bicarbonate and a piece of tinfoil about 10cm square. Bring to the boil and put silverware in for a few seconds or until clean. Remove with tongs.

700.

To make a cheap degreasant for bicycles, car engines etc mix 1 gallon (3.8 L) of water with a cup (240 ml) of ammonia, half a cup (120 ml) of vinegar, and a quarter cup (60 ml) of baking soda. Stir together well.

701.

If your vacuum cleaner has died, or you want to save on energy costs, consider doing

without. Wooden floors can be cleaned easily with a broom or mop, and carpets with a cheap carpet sweeper. Rugs can be beaten outdoors with a large flat object like a frying pan or old tennis racket. It's good exercise!

702.

Used coffee grounds will clean and degrease pots and pans, saving you money on washing up liquid.

703.

Pet hairs can be removed from carpets with a rubber broom; it's cheaper than vacuuming.

704.

Equal parts of vinegar and olive oil, rubbed well in, will remove white rings from furniture.

705.

A squeezed lemon can be used to shine mirrors and chrome; simply rub on then polish off with a clean cloth.

Gardens and growing

706.

Grow fruit and vegetables if you have a garden. You can save huge amounts of money this way, without too much effort. Choose hardy fruit and vegetables which don't need much attention once planted, such as potatoes, kale, rhubarb, raspberries, beans, chard, carrots, salad mix etc. Fruit trees are worth it if you intend to stay in the same house for years; they don't need watering or much maintenance.

707.

You don't need a garden to grow things. Herbs, sprouts etc can be grown indoors or on windowsills.

708.

No need to buy a watering can for window boxes, balcony plants etc. Simply punch small holes in the lid of an old plastic milk bottle or water bottle.

709.

Don't throw away old shoelaces. They can be used as wicks for plant watering. If you are away for a few days, simply put one end of the shoelace an inch or so into the soil of a pot plant. Put the other end right down into the bottom of a one litre plastic bottle of water. The lace acts like a wick, bringing water into the plant at a steady rate via capillary action. Your plants may not get as much water as they need to thrive, but they will usually get enough to stay alive.

710.

Use cardboard tubes from toilet rolls as pots for seedlings (fold the bottom half of the tube inwards first). This will biodegrade in soil.

711.

Don't spend money on weedkillers. At the end of winter, cover weedy ground with layers of newspaper, cardboard or carpet up to about ½ an inch thick. Cut holes for where you want to plant shrubs or flowers. Dampen slightly then add clean top soil, remembering to mark the areas you've planted. The weeds will be choked off by the covering, but the plants will thrive.

712.

The water that vegetables, pulses, rice etc has been boiled in can be used as nutritious plant food when cooled.

713.

Cats are said to dislike the smell of vinegar; spray some around areas that you want cats to avoid.

714.

Old plastic garden furniture can be given a new lease of life by repainting. A special type of paint for flexible plastic is available from DIY stores – ordinary paint is likely to flake off. For a really nice look paint on a light brown base coat then a darker wood grain effect on top.

715.

A small amount of sugar and vinegar added to water in a vase will help flowers live longer.

716.

Half a cup of salt and half a cup of washing up liquid in a gallon of vinegar makes cheap weedkiller.

717.

Wood ash can be sprinkled on snowy paths and drives to help traction and avoid slips.

718.

Change vase water daily to preserve the freshness of cut flowers.

719.

Pick herbs in summer to dry for winter use. Simply tie a bunch together and hang it up somewhere dry and airy. When it is dry, put it on a big sheet of newspaper and scrape off all the leaves, then pour into an airtight jar. With some herbs, such as mint, you can use the stalks also if finely cut.

720.

Cheap shiny plastic garden tubs and boxes can be made to look like terracotta by sanding lightly with sandpaper then painting on live yoghurt with a a paintbrush; this encourages mould and lichen growth for an antique look.

721.

Plant food can be made for free by soaking nettles in water for four weeks or so. The infusion then makes a nutritious fertilizer.

722.

Cut the top half of a clear plastic drinks bottle to make a cloche for seedlings (remember to leave the cap off.)

723.

Polystyrene packing chips can be reused by putting them in the bottom of plant pots under the soil. This helps the pot drain more easily.

724.

Avoid disposal fees for scrap concrete and rubble after building projects; break them up to make a rockery for the garden.

725.

Keeping chickens can be a fun hobby especially for children, and provides an almost free source of eggs.

726.

Cut up yoghurt pots into strips about one inch wide and cut a point at the end. Use the blank side as labels for your flowerbeds, pots etc so you remember what seeds you've planted. Use a permanent marker.

727.

Preserve your houseplants by putting them outside in the garden (out of full sunlight) when you're on holiday. If you're in the UK, there will usually be enough rain to keep them healthy.

728.

Don't buy slug pellets. Slugs can be killed easily by using traps baited with beer. Around your garden vegetable plot, bury a used yoghurt pot so that the rim is level with the ground, then put a little stale beer in. The slugs are attracted to the beer and fall in, then can't get out.

729.

Save money on herbs by growing your own at home. Plants bought from outdoor garden centres are usually longer lasting than the kind you get in supermarkets.

730.

Don't buy ties for plants etc. Simply cut up old tights and use instead; the material is strong and long lasting.

731.

Save uncooked food waste for compost. This will save money on expensive fertilisers for your garden.

732.

Use old car tyres to plant potatoes. Fill the hole with soil and plant your seed potatoes. As they grow, add more tyres and soil.

733.

Don't waste money on bean sprouts from shops. It's easy to grow your own indoors at any time of year. Simply soak a handful of mung beans overnight, then place in an old yoghurt pot in which you have punched a few drainage holes. Fill the pot twice a day and allow to drain. In a few days you will have small, crisp, delicious beanshoots for stirfries, sandwiches, salads etc.

734.

Use hanging baskets to grow strawberries in the garden on or on a balcony. Slugs and snails can't get to them.

735.

Boiling water mixed with salt is said to work as a weedkiller. Don't use on areas where wanted plants are growing.

736.

Lemon balm (*Melissa officinalis*) is easy to grow in the garden or can be bought cheaply in dried form. It makes a cheap lemon substitute in many drinks and recipes.

737.

Bury broken eggshells in a ring around plants (sharp points facing out of the soil) to deter slugs and snails. This also has a fertilizing effect.

738.

Lolly sticks (popsicle sticks) can be saved for plant labels.

739.

Don't throw away sprouted potatoes. They can be planted in soil to grow more potatoes.

740.

A cheap alternative to wellingtons in the garden – just tie plastic bags round your ordinary shoes.

741.

Get a water butt for the garden if you're on a water meter. Some councils offer these at reduced cost.

742.

Used coffee grounds are said to act as a repellent to slugs, snails and cats around vegetable plots, flower beds etc.

743.

Don't throw away a sprouted onion. Place it in a bulb jar by a window and the sprouts will grow. These can be harvested and eaten like chives.

744.

If you don't have a bulb jar, the bulb can be suspended in the water of a jam jar. Stick three toothpicks into the side of the bulb to suspend it from the rim of the jar, ensuring that the base of the bulb sits in the water.

745.

A sprouted onion can also be planted in soil; it will produce attractive flowers.

746.

Horse manure can make good free fertilizer for the garden. If you live near stables, ask if they will let you take some.

747.

Wood ashes are said to repel garden pests such as slugs and snails if sprinkled around troubled areas.

748.

Old car tyres make great garden planter pots; for a stylish look paint them with white paint or terracotta stone effect paint.

749.

A wormery (a sealed box containing live worms) will turn all your kitchen waste, cooked and uncooked, into very good liquid fertilizer and will pay for itself quickly.

750.

If you don't have a garden, ask your council if allotments are available for rent in your area.

751.

Can't get an allotment? Try garden sharing. Ask around online or via your local community centre, church etc whether anyone is willing for you to start a vegetable patch in their garden, either in return for a share of produce or for helping with general upkeep in their garden. This could be a great help to an elderly person.

752.

Yoghurt pots make ideal plant pots for small plants etc. For a better look, cover them with Fablon or wrapping paper (for indoor use) or paint with a terracotta paint.

753.

Another method to make cheap plastic garden items look better is to mix sand with matt stone coloured paint. When applied this gives a rough stone finish to smooth plastic.

754.

If you have very weedy garden soil which chokes plants, submerge large plant pots to about one or two inches above ground level and fill them with good soil and compost. This will protect your plants from weeds as they grow, and the rim of the pot will protect against slugs and other pests. Once the plants grows big and strong enough, just level off the soil to hide the edge of the pot.

755.

Don't throw away a leaky flower vase. Simply put a freezer bag inside and top the bag up with water.

756.

Unwanted CDs can be used as bird scarers for the garden. Simply hang them on threads from garden canes. Birds are said to dislike the dazzling effect.

757.

A quarter of a teaspoon of bleach per litre of water in vases is said to prolong the life of cut flowers.

758.

Water cress is easy to grow indoors and provides a cheap and easy flavouring for soups and sandwiches.

759.

The water that eggs have been boiled in, once cooled, makes a cheap and nutritious plant food.

760.

Always cover garden furniture when not in use. Cheap opaque plastic sheeting from pound shops will do the trick. Exposure to the elements, even in summer, will wear out garden furniture (even plastic) more quickly.

761.

If you don't have a garden, leave pot plants in bowls of water or in a couple of inches of water in the bath when you go on holiday.

762.

Go foraging. Blackberries and nettles are the easiest plants to start with. Ramsons (wild garlic) also grow in profusion in the UK. Richard Mabey's pocket book *Food for Free* will pay for itself many times over. Every time you go out for a walk in the country, take a couple of carrier bags or plastic containers as you never know what you might find.

763.

Don't spend money on canes for plants; a walk in any woodland area will provide you with windfall sticks whenever you need them.

764.

The large clear plastic boxes with holes in the bottom that mushrooms etc are sold in can be inverted to use as propagating boxes for seedlings.

Shopping and bargains

765.

Use cash only, it will help you keep track of your spending more easily.

766.

Use charity shops/thrift stores but don't just go when you need something – you rarely find it. Instead, make regular trips to see what's available. But remember – only buy something that you really need!

767.

If you normally drive to the shops, then walk or cycle instead. You'll only buy what you can carry and will save on fuel. Only do this if your local shops aren't more expensive than the supermarket. A rucksack or a wheeled shopping bag is useful for this.

768.

Be careful with coupons. It might seem like money saving, but many are for expensive branded products and are designed to make you think you're saving money when you're paying too much in the first place.

769.

For cheap staple foods visit ethnic supermarkets such as Indian or Chinese run-businesses. They often have large bags of rice, lentils etc at low prices.

770.

Go 'shopping' in the cupboard/freezer to use up old items.

771.

Always check price per unit of measurement. Supermarkets sometimes trick you into thinking you're getting more for your money when you're not.

772.

Most charity shops in the UK won't sell used electrical items. However, some charities have engineers who volunteer to check goods are safe. Ask at your local charity shop for the address of the branches they work for.

773.

When buying small items in the supermarket, check carefully that they have been packed after being paid for. It's easy for them to roll away and get lost in the hustle of a big queue.

774.

High priced goods are often stocked at eye level on supermarket shelves. Check low down and high up for bargains.

775.

If you live in a rural area, save on trips to the supermarket by pooling a weekly online shop with neighbours. This will negate the delivery charge and means everyone will save on fuel or bus fares.

776.

If you need a particular item, put the word out to friends and relations on social media. Offer to pay up to a certain amount as a courtesy.You'll be surprised how often people (sometimes even friends of friends) have a suitable item that they're happy to get rid of for nothing.

777.

Cheap articles can be bought online at police auctions, where stolen property which has not been claimed is sold. Try www.bumblebeeauctions.co.uk

778.

Sign up for the Facebook pages of any local churches, charities, youth groups etc; that way you will be kept informed if they are holding a jumble sale, yard sale, bazaar etc.

779.

If you regularly buy items in bulk online, check out Amazon's 'subscribe and save' programme for savings.

780.

If you shop weekly, leave the shopping a day later each week. This will give you a week's 'free' shopping every eight weeks.

781.

Keep a small list of items that you need but not urgently. Carry this in your purse and wallet to consult if you are passing a charity shop/car boot sale/yard sale etc.

782.

Check if your borough or city holds street cleansing days when residents can put out large items on the street for disposal. Get to know these days and, the night before, take a stroll around the area. People often throw away perfectly good items of furniture, household goods etc. It's polite (and in some places a legal obligation) to ask the householder first if you can take something.

783.

Supermarkets sometimes put newer items at the back of the shelves; compare the use by dates of items at the front and back of the shelves before buying.

784.

Don't be afraid to politely ask if a lower price can be offered at car boot sales, secondhand shops etc (although it's bad form to haggle in charity shops). If you're too shy to ask, sometimes just expressing interest in the item then walking away will result in a lower offer being made.

785.

To save money on electrical items such as hi fis, TVs etc try the Cash Convertors chain of shops. They often have second-hand 'big ticket' items at low prices as well as computer games, DVDs etc

786.

A general moneysaving rule is to buy a product in dried or concentrated form where possible. It is usually cheaper; with ready made products you are often just paying for added water and extra packaging.

787.

Keep an inventory of what food you have at home. This will prevent unnecessary spending in the shops.

788.

Try charity shops/thrift stores run by local charities rather than the national chains, often these have lower prices and better bargains.

789.

Always check the price in terms of weight and volume when buying things; eg, how much do you actually get for your money? Manufacturers use all kinds of tricks such as bulky packaging, large bottles etc to make you think you're getting more for your money.

790.

Most military surplus companies use a grading system to denote the quality of their goods, from new to heavily used. Make sure you check how your item is graded before ordering online.

791.

When considering whether to buy something, look at the price in terms of your hourly income. Would you work those hours to pay for it?

792.

Get to know your local dump. People often throw away perfectly good items which the staff will salvage and either give away or sell cheaply. One man I know never buys a new inner tube if he gets a puncture on his bike – he just goes to the dump and gets a whole new wheel!

793.

Ask at your local charity shop/thrift store if they have regular sale days. If so, put them in your diary and drop by on those days.

794.

Non-perishable staples like soap, toilet paper etc should always be bought in the biggest amounts possible, assuming you have storage space which can't be put to more profitable use. They won't lose their value over time – unlike money in the bank!

795.

Carry a basket in the supermarket instead of pushing a trolley, you will only buy what you need and will be less tempted to toss items in.

796.

Sign up for Freecycle. (www.freecycle.org) This online community is a good source of completely free articles of all kinds.

797.

Always check out the reduced section at the supermarket. Food close to its sell by date can be frozen and kept for later. Some supermarkets have a set time and day for putting out reduced items, but don't often like to publicise it. Try asking a shelf stacker rather than a manager.

798.

Military surplus suppliers online or in the high street can be a source of amazing bargains in camping and survival equipment, footwear and practical, hard wearing clothing.

799.

When bidding on Ebay, wait until the last hour of the auction before bidding. Decide your maximum bid in advance and set Ebay's controls so that the system will bid automatically for you up to that amount.

800.

Buy postage stamps in bulk. British first and second class stamps do not have the value marked on them and can still be used even after prices have gone up.

801.

Set up a grocery buying club with friends and family. Pool your money in order to buy staple items in bulk at large discounts.

802.

Make a shopping list and keep to it, you will spend less.

803.

If you don't have time to make a list, take a quick picture of your fridge and/or larder with your phone so that you can check what you have while shopping.

804.

Set up a reminder on Ebay for any items you need. Eg, if you are looking for something like a child's winter coat for age 7-9 costing less than £10, you can set this up as a search and any time one is for sale, you will be sent a notification email.

805.

Take a tape measure when you go shopping to check sizes against your family sizes list. The free paper ones from IKEA are ideal.

806.

Carry sizes of your family members in your purse or wallet. That way if you see a bargain in a charity shop/thrift store etc you'll know if it's the right size. Remember to keep children's sizes – and adult waist sizes – up to date!

807.

Shop at car boot sales or jumble sales just before the end; the organisers are usually keen to get rid of their stuff and will often accept lower offers.

808.

If your spouse or family members are fussy about brands, try mixing generic products with branded products, or putting generic products like cereal into branded boxes. Usually they won't notice the difference.

809.

If your workplace often holds lunch meetings, get to know the staff who deal with the catering.

Often, large amounts of good quality food gets left uneaten at business lunches, only to be thrown away afterwards.

Moneysaving around the house

810.

Always turn your mattress when changing your sheets. This distributes wear and makes the mattress last much longer. An easy way to do it is to pencil in a number on every corner of the mattress in a sequence from 1 to 8. Each time you change the sheets, turn the mattress so that the next number in the sequence is always showing on the top right hand corner of the mattress by the bedhead. This way you will always distribute wear evenly.

811.

Egg cartons are useful for organised storage of screws, buttons, odds and ends etc of similar types and can easily be stacked.

812.

Long cords from broken electrical appliances can be cut off and used as strong rope for washing lines in a small garden, tieing back plants etc.

813.

Collect all the odd coins around the house in jars, down the back of the sofa, etc. You may be surprised just how much is lying around.

814.

Children's crayons can be used to cover up scratches in wooden furniture and work in the same way as expensive scratch cover wax kits.

815.

Before spending money on software check online to see if free equivalent software is available. This is not pirated but genuine software such as VLC Media Player. If in doubt if software is genuine, Google the name to see if any scam reports come up.

816.

For cheap but unusual wall decorations, try Victorian engravings, which are available quite cheaply online. Often you can find one of your town or city. Put in a charity shop/thrift store picture frame.

817.

Many carpet showrooms, DIY shops etc will sell offcuts of lino cheaply. These can be used to make great hardwearing counter top covers or chair seat covers for worn furniture. Alternatively, pound shops/dollar stores often sell self adhesive vinyl tiles very cheaply which can be used in the same way .

818.

A flint and steel (fire striker) for fire lighting will last many years and can't get wet or broken on camping trips.

819.

Don't buy expensive ant killing chemicals; boiling water poured into nests and areas of infestation will kill them.

820.

If you have a dehumidifier, save the water for use in your steam iron or steam cleaner; it is distilled and will prolong the life of the appliances.

821.

Plaster filler in powder form costs less than made up versions, and can be stored longer.

822.

Save yoghurt pots and jam jars for the garden shed/workshop, they are ideal for storing nails and screws, soaking paintbrushes etc.

823.

The glass plate from a microwave can be used as a serving dish.

824.

The large charity shop/thrift store chains sometimes have furniture warehouses with low priced second hand furniture too big to fit in high street shops. Check with your local branch or online to find out.

825.

Vintage newspapers, maps, old comics or sheet music can make interesting wallpaper for a small room such as a downstairs loo. Paste on with wallpaper paste and then varnish over with polyurethane varnish.

826.

Bring an old glue stick back to life by rubbing a little water into the hardened glue.

827.

For sanding jobs wire wool can be cheaper than using sandpaper and is just as effective.

828.

New candles can be made from the stubs of old ones and bits of wax from candlesticks. Cut up the old stubs into pieces and remove the wicks. Melt down in an old saucepan. Use a jam jar for a mould, but first, run a length of cotton string or twine through the hot wax. When it cools, tie it round a pencil and suspend the wick into the jam jar. Pour the hot wax into the jam jar and allow to cool, then untie the wick from the pencil and trim to size.

829.

Broken appliance? It could just be a minor problem you can fix yourself. Check technical forums online, such as those at Moneysaving Expert, for free and helpful advice. Never open up electrical appliances if you are not qualified.

830.

Gaffer tape (also known as elephant tape or duct tape) is invaluable for all kinds of repair around the home. Avoid the cheap type from pound shops/dollar stores as this is not as strong as the well known brands.

831.

No need to spend money on an indoor clothes airer. A stout hook or screw between the doorframe and the window frame will enable you to rig up an indoor clothesline (available cheaply from pound shops/dollar stores). It's easily taken down when not in use. If you need more drying space just add more lines.

832.

Broken roller runner in a chest of drawers? Don't pay for a replacement which will probably just break again. Just remove the old rollers and cut to size four pieces of softwood about 1' wide. Using wood glue, fix these to the inside of the chest above and below where the drawer will go.

Do a test run first using gaffer tape to stick the runners in the right place, then mark the position carefully with pencil. Lubricate lightly with candle wax for a smooth action. There will be no 'stop' to prevent the drawer falling out when pulled too far – but you can make one simply by fixing the drawer to the back of the chest with a piece of twine or old shoelace.

833.

Get as much paint as possible off paint brushes by wiping them on newspaper and old rags; this way you use less brush cleaning fluid.

834.

Old blankets or can be made into draft excluders for doors. Simply cut to size, roll tightly and safety pin or tack stitch in place. Old towels work better for window sills, as they will absorb condensation better.

835.

Alternatively choose a popular crockery design such as Woods Ware Green Beryl which is widely available second hand when you require replacement pieces.

836.

Don't throw away white spirit that you have used to soak paintbrushes in. Leave it for a week or so until the paint sinks to the bottom, then pour off into a new container for re-use.

837.

If you are throwing away scrap timber etc, remove screws and nails for re-use.

838.

If you're throwing out a front loading washing machine, remove the window first. It makes a great serving bowl for salads etc.

839.

Save money on glue. Make a simple paper glue with half a cup of the cheapest white flour and one third of a cup of water. Apply using a paint brush and store in a jam jar in the fridge.

840.

Shells and colourful pebbles collected from the beach and put in a bowl make a pretty, free ornament for the bathroom.

841.

Broken rubber bands can be tied with a reef knot and reused.

842.

Hang essential oils on a facecloth over your radiator for a cheap room freshener.

843.

Buying new carpets? Manmade carpets will last much longer than wool, are easier to clean, less prone to fading, won't be eaten by moths, and cost considerably less.

844.

Home made fly paper can be easily and cheaply made by smearing scrap paper with Vaseline. Hang up in the areas troubled by flies.

845.

Candle stubs can be used as firelighters in open fires or stoves.

846.

Cut thin slices from old wine corks to use as pads under vases etc to prevent damage to furniture. Affix with glue or for a temporary fix, use blutac.

847.

Cut strips from old rubber gloves to make sturdy elastic bands.

848.

Don't throw out old, worn melamine furniture or kitchen units. These can be brought back to life cheaply and easily. Use melamine primer (from DIY shops) to paint the furniture. Then any kind of paint can usually be used on top of the primer. This works particularly well with fresh, matt pastel colours like cream or French Grey. For the final touch add some new handles and knobs.

849.

It's always worth having a supply of plastic cable ties around the house. They are invaluable for tricky mending and binding jobs.

850.

Save money on printer cartridges with a re-inking kit, available from computer shops, stationers or online. Results vary for colour printing, but for black and white printing they usually work well.

851.

Skips can be a good source of scrap timber and building materials for home projects. Always ask the homeowner before taking something, but they'll usually be glad to let you have it as it will keep their costs down too.

852.

Use a knife or letter opener to open post carefully so that you can save the envelope for re-use.

853.

Always remove the plugs from electrical appliances if you are throwing them out; they can be reused.

854.

Dried orange peel makes good kindling for the fireplace and smells pleasant.

855.

Junk mail envelopes and the backs of leaflets etc make good notepads to keep by the phone.

856.

Save money on room freshener plug ins; an oil burner with a tealight and essential oil will work just as well and last much longer.

857.

Strong pepper sprinkled around makes a cheap deterrent against rats or mice in garages, basements etc.

858.

Toothpaste makes a quick and cheap filler for small holes in plaster, great for covering up holes in walls made by nails or drawing pins. This is a good tip for people in rented accommodation.

859.

A cigarette lighter that has run out of gas can be kept to light gas stoves, if the flint is still working.

860.

Dental floss (the unflavoured kind) can be used to cut soft cakes very easily.

861.

If a plug fuse blows, save money on a new one by using one from an appliance you don't use often. (Always ensure the amperage is correct). Keep the plug of the disused appliance disassembled or clearly marked, so that you remember it does not have a fuse.

862.

Old newspapers can be used in place of lining paper for walls; simply paste on then paint over with emulsion. Don't use recently printed newspaper as the ink can leach through the paint.

863.

Save on printer ink by using an ink saving program such as Preton Saver, Inkgard or Ecofont. Once installed, these instruct your printer to use less ink. As with all programs check carefully before downloading to make sure your computer is compatible.

864.

Take your shoes off indoors and change to slippers; this will save wear and tear on carpets and help your shoes last longer too.

865.

When printing from your computer, always print double sided or reuse paper which is blank on one side.

866.

A great space saver for the garden shed: Nail jam jar lids to the ceiling beams. Then fill the jar with screws, nails etc. Simply screw into the lid for space-saving storage when not in use.

867.

Don't buy rubber bands. Postmen often leave them on your front path or on the pavement; just pick them up and wash clean for reuse.

868.

Reuse printer paper by printing on both sides. If paper is torn or creased, use the blank side for notepads instead.

869.

If you have a gas cooker, save used matches in a dish by the cooker. If you have one hob already lit and need to light another, simply use a spent match as a spill to light the other hob.

870.

Refresh lavender bags that have gone stale by rubbing them or adding lavender essence.

871.

Scratches on wooden furniture can be covered with a walnut. Simply rub the nut over the scratch then buff with a cloth. Natural oils in the nut will cover the scratch.

872.

Tired furniture, especially cheap and nasty 1970s melamine furniture, can be given an antique makeover with wood grain paint kits, such as Ronseal Paint and Grain, available from DIY shops. Put a coat of varnish on top and add antique style fittings to give it a really smart look.

873.

Using bubble wrap by the roll inside a brown paper envelope is usually cheaper than buying jiffy bags.

874.

An old glossy magazine makes a good mousemat – it has a smooth surface and doesn't cost anything.

875.

Epoxy modelling clay is useful for odd little repairs around the home. Brand names include 'Milliput'. It is cheap and can be worked like plasticine but sets hard as stone and can be used to repair metal, porcelain etc.

876.

Make new candles from candle stubs and wax drippings. This works best with candles of a similar type. Remove the wicks and places in an old tin can. Put the tin can in a saucepan of water and heat until the wax is liquid. Use an old jam jar for a mould. Stretch a rubber band across the top of the jar and tie a piece of string round it long enough to reach to the bottom of the jar (this will be the wick). Then carefully pour the hot wax into the jar and leave to set.

877.

A pencil stub holder/pencil extender (available online) will extend the lives of your pencils by enabling you to use them right to the end.

878.

Don't throw away jiffy bags, brown envelopes etc. Simply paste clean paper over the address area and stamp area then reuse.

879.

If you have a threadbare carpet and can't afford to replace it, use matt oil paint or fabric paint to exactly match the colour of the material, and paint over the threadbare area. This works particularly well on worn stair carpets.

880.

Rusty screw or other metal component? Simply soak overnight in white vinegar or coca-cola to remove rust.

881.

Set your printer to print in black and white as a default setting, to avoid wasting colour ink.

882.

Tired kitchen counters, kitchen table tops, chair seats etc can be revitalised quickly and cheaply with Fablon, a self adhesive plastic material in all kinds of designs such as granite, marble etc.

883.

Use up the last drops of paint in a paint tin, and clean your brush off, by painting the outside of the tin. When it's dried it will be a useful plant pot or open storage tin.

884.

A worn out table top can be refreshed cheaply and quickly by covering with green baize fabric. This works well with old fashioned tables that are used as writing desks etc. just fold and tuck in neatly on the underside of the table top and secure with drawing pins or tacks. It can be removed if necessary for washing.

885.

Don't throw away wet wipes which have dried out in the packet. Simply add a little water to the packet, seal up and they will be good as new in a couple of hours.

886.

If you smoke or light fires regularly, disposable lighters are cheaper than matches in the long run. Boxes of 50 can be purchased online for about ten pounds. A disposable lighter will give up to 3,000 lights.

887.

Save money on computers with a reconditioned model. These are secondhand but have been checked by engineers. They are considerably cheaper than new models. Stores such as PC World stock them.

888.

Sharpen the blades of dull scissors by rubbing them with a little wire wool.

889.

Use an envelope or jar system for saving small amounts of money; mark the envelopes with labels such as 'holiday; 'pub', 'cinema', 'petrol' etc and set aside regular amounts.

890.

Cold green tea, very strong and sweetened with sugar, when set about the room in saucers, is said to attract flies and destroy them.

891.

A clean shell or pebble in a kettle is said to keep limescale at bay through chemical attraction; and will make your kettle last longer.

892.

Dental floss makes a very strong thread for repairing items such as bag linings, leather items etc.

893.

If a room is out of use for a long period of time, keep the curtains closed and cover the furniture, paintings etc with old sheets. Sunlight, even in mild climates, will eventually fade and damage things.

894.

Old socks can be used for lavender bags as a moth repellent in wardrobes. Fill with cut and dried lavender and hang from the rail with ribbon.

895.

Save the shiny backing paper from adhesive labels such as Amazon book labels etc. Put a small piece under the end of a roll of sellotape. It will help you find the end of the roll and can be peeled off next time you use it. Unlike the usual method of folding the tape back on itself, will not waste any of it.

896.

Telescopic shower curtain rails (tension rods) can be used at windows as well, if the window frame is not flush with the wall. This saves time and money on expensive rails and fittings, especially if you live in rented accommodation.

897.

When buying crockery, choose a plain and simple white design. This will be easier to replace when pieces get broken, and small chips will not be seen as easily as with coloured crockery.

898.

Cardboard tubes from toilet rolls can be stacked vertically in drawers and used as organisers for socks, tights, cables etc.

899.

A stapleless stapler (which works by punching and folding a tab in sheets of paper) is inexpensive and save on staples in the long run.

900.

Don't throw away old dried paint brushes or pay for expensive brush restorer fluid. Just soak them in white vinegar for an hour then simmer them in a saucepan of white vinegar until good as new.

901.

If you have heavily patterned carpets you don't like, but can't afford to replace them, a cheap and quick trick is to buy a large, plain rug to act as a centrepiece in the room. This will draw attention away from the rest of the carpet. You can sometimes buy large offcuts of plain carpet from showrooms; simply add braiding to the rough edges using fabric glue for a professional look.

902.

Save money on bin liners with a 'two bin bag' system. Put 'wet' rubbish in your kitchen bin and throw the bag away when you empty the bin. Put 'dry' rubbish in a bin liner next to the bin. Simply empty that bag into your outside bin and reuse.

903.

Shabby white goods (fridges, washing machines etc) can be made to look as good as new with ordinary gloss paint. Clean well with sugar soap and remove any rust spots with wire wool. Paint with a fine brush and 'feather' the brush (use it very lightly) to give a professional finish. This can also be used to match your white goods to your decor.

904.

Use an old plastic bottle to make a fly trap. Cut the bottle in half and invert the top half into the bottom, sealing the edge with sellotape. Pour some honey or fizzy pop into the bottle. The flies will crawl in but won't be able to get out.

905.

Candle stubs can be used as lubricant for sticky drawers, doors etc.

Bills, utilities and energy saving

906.

Consider putting curtains on your front door. This stops hallways feeling draughty and will cut down on heating bills.

907.

It sounds obvious, but remember to keep the doors and window shut in any room in which you have AC running. Keeping windows and doors open, even internal doors, uses up much more energy.

908.

To cool your house without air conditioning, open windows and doors early in the morning to let the cool air in, then keep doors, windows and curtains closed after mid morning to shut the heat out. Leave a window in a shaded position open a little to provide ventilation. If you have sash windows, keep the top sash open a little as well to allow hot air (which rises) to escape.

909.

To keep cool in hot weather without air conditioning, use a cooling scarf or a cooling cushion. These are available online and can be worn or sat on to cool you down in hot weather.

910.

If possible keep your fridge out of direct sunlight and in a cool place such as an outhouse; it will use less energy to keep cool.

911.

When your car or house insurance comes up for renewal, shop around using comparison sites. If you get a better offer but would like to stay with your current insurer, discuss it with them on the phone, sometimes they will reduce your quote.

912.

If you are self employed, investigate possible tax breaks, particularly if you work from home. Things like clothing, electricity and computer costs can sometimes be offset against tax.

913.

Use your dishwasher on an economy cycle if it has one.

914.

Email instead of call, if you're on a pay as you go phone package.

915.

If you're chilly on the sofa, use a hot water bottle and blanket to keep warm. Microwave hot water bottles are cheaper and safer, but be careful when using them in small microwaves as they need to rotate freely.

916.

Turn down the cooling on your AC by a few degrees; you should aim for just a couple of degrees cooler than the outside air.

917.

A cold outside wall in a room can be insulated using expanded polystyrene wallpaper; this is pasted on like normal wallpaper and can then be papered over with lining paper.

918.

Make sure your fridge is not pushed up against a wall. A gap to ensure air circulation will use less energy.

919.

Open and shut the fridge door as quickly as possible. Spending a long time looking inside the fridge with the door open uses more power.

920.

Feeling cold? Don't turn up the heating. Just go for a quick walk round the block. The exercise will warm you up and the house will feel warmer when you come back in.

921.

If you receive a pay rise at work (we live in hope...) put the amount of the increase in your savings account every month, by direct debit.

922.

Turn down the heating. If you do this gradually over the course of a few days, it is less noticeable than a sudden change.

923.

Fill a one litre plastic bottle with water and put it in the toilet cistern to save water when you flush. You can also use a brick but these can disintegrate over time and cause blockages.

924.

If you live in a hot climate try using a solar cooker. This will cook your food for free and can be made from scrap items around the home. See online for further details.

925.

Turn off lights and any appliances around the house. Even small appliances on standby use electricity which all adds up over time.

926.

For free hot water in summer, use a camping solar shower. This is basically a large plastic bag which you hang up in the sun all day for heated water by the evening. It works best in sunny climates.

927.

If you live in a hot climate save fuel costs with 'dashboard cooking' to bake biscuits, cakes or bread. Simply place your items on a baking tray and place on your dashboard with the car parked in full sun. Temperatures inside the car can be sufficient for baking.

928.

Turn off the lights or just use a small light when watching TV; it saves power and feels more like the cinema. Be careful about doing this when using a computer however as it can cause eyestrain.

929.

Be sure to close the curtains as soon as dusk falls to trap more heat in the room.

930.

Keep the fridge full, with bottles of water if necessary. A full fridge (as long as it is not full to bursting) is said to use less energy to cool.

931.

Save on heating by turning the heating off at least half an hour before you plan to go out. The house will still be warm. Don't turn on heating again until you've been in for half an hour and have started to notice the difference in temperature.

932.

Garden awnings/gazebos are available quite cheaply from shops like Argos. If you have a ground floor window or French doors in direct sunlight, keep the gazebo up against it to provide shade and keep the room cool.

933.

If you have an open fire, a briquette maker can be used to make logs from old newspapers, scrap paper etc.

934.

Turn the central heating off completely at night. You don't need it when you're in bed.

935.

Get to know how much electricity your appliances use. General Electric offers rough estimates here:

http://visualization.geblogs.com/visualization/appliances/

This way you can calculate how much you are spending each time you use an appliance.

936.

If you have a ceiling fan, check if it runs in reverse (blowing air downwards). Hot air rises, so this is a cheap way of keeping the room warm in winter.

937.

Turn the tap off when brushing your teeth.

938.

Heavy cloth pinned or taped over the letter box and keyhole on your front door will cut down on draughts. Try it on catflaps too.

939.

If you don't want to pay for heavy curtains to keep winter drafts out, you can make insulating liners cheaply and easily using old blankets. Cut to size if necessary (using pinking shears) and use safety pins and curtain hooks to attach them to the hooks of your existing curtains. The lining will not be seen from inside the room and can easily be removed when winter is over.

940.

Unless you have an auto-defrost fridge, make sure it is defrosted regularly to save on power.

941.

If all else fails, a cheap way to keep cool, for example while reading, is to sit in a cold bath!

942.

If buying a fan heater, buy one with a 'fan only' function. This can be used to keep you cool in summer.

943.

Buy rechargeable batteries and a charger. It saves money in the long run and is better for the environment.

944.

Keep cool on hot nights without spending money on AC, by cooling your bed down with a couple of those blue plastic cooling bricks for picnic hampers. One in the bed and one under the pillow will do the trick.

945.

Spend more time reading in your public library, perhaps one evening a week in winter. This will save on heating and lighting costs.

946.

Clean the condenser coils on the back of your fridge every so often to improve efficiency.

947.

Keep a large jug or pot by the kitchen sink to collect water when running the tap to warm it up etc. Use to water plants or pour into water butt in the garden.

948.

Thermal underwear and hiking socks will keep you toasty in winter, saving on fuel bills. If you don't want to pay for thermal underwear, tights or pyjama bottoms under your trousers will work also.

949.

In the UK, free loft insulation may be available from the government or your local council. Check online for latest deals. This can save huge amounts in energy bills.

950.

Not using your electric blanket? Put it on the sofa while you're on – no need to heat the rest of the room.

951.

Always check bank and credit card statements carefully and don't hesitate to report anything that you can't remember paying for – better safe than sorry.

952.

A will doesn't always have to be made by a lawyer. Check the internet for laws in your state/country; in some places it is legal to draw up a will yourself.

953.

Make sure you have a blanket under your bottom bedsheet for extra warmth. In really cold bedrooms an old duvet can be used instead of a blanket; this works best with a stretch fitted sheet.

954.

Play a DVD of an open fireplace on your TV (or watch one on youtube on your computer). It can give a feeling of warmth in a cold room, and costs nothing.

955.

Use a plug-in LED nightlight in areas such as hallways etc which don't need much light. This uses less electricity than an overhead light.

956.

Cool your house in summer with homemade blinds. Simply cut flattened cardboard boxes to size (you can use gaffer tape to fix sections together) and cover one side with tinfoil. Hang them from hooks on the window frame (if you have Upvc windows you can get self adhesive hooks from pound shops/dollar stores). In summer, place the tinfoil side facing outwards, and this will deflect the sun's glare and keep the room cool and shady.

You can cut slits in the cardboard to allow a little light in. In winter, put the tinfoil side facing into the room to reflect heat back. If you're aesthetically minded, keep the curtains closed over the cardboard to keep it out of sight.

957.

In cold weather after cooking vegetables don't pour the water away, leave it out until it cools, to warm the kitchen.

958.

To save energy, only boil the amount of water you need in the kettle. The easiest way to do this is to fill your mug or teapot with water then pour it into the kettle.

959.

Always fix dripping taps. If you can't, keep a pot or pan under it to save the water.

960.

Lightly dusting your skin with cornstarch is said to make you feel cooler in very hot humid weather.

961.

Put tinfoil behind radiators to reflect heat out of the wall and back into the room. Pasting tinfoil to sheets of cardboard will make the job easier.

962.

Batteries that have run out in large appliances can still sometimes work in items which don't use much power, such as remote controls, clocks etc.

963.

Try turning your fridge down to save power. Fridges should be set at about 3 to 5C (37 to 41F) (Source: Wikipedia). Use an ordinary household thermometer to check the temperature.

964.

Keep your credit card frozen in a lump of ice in the freezer. That way it can be defrosted when really needed, but can't be used casually.

965.

Save cooking costs with a haybox or 'fireless cooker'. This is an insulated box which can be made easily at home. You bring cooking to the boil and then put the pot in the box, allowing it to cook in its own heat without paying for any more fuel. Take a box, cardboard or wooden, line it with several layers of newspapers either pasted or tacked on. Nearly fill it with hay, sawdust, old cloths or duvets or crumpled paper. Leave a space where you will set your pan. Pack the filling as tight as you can around the pan, and leave to cook. Lots of youtube videos and information is online.

966.

If you are retired, consider long-term holiday deals in southern European destinations such as Spain or Malta (or Florida or Mexico if you live in the US or Canada). It can sometimes work out more cheaply to spend the coldest part of the winter abroad than to pay for your heating and lighting.

967.

Want to feel cooler without cranking up the AC? Go outside in the heat for a few minutes' walk; when you come back inside your relatively cooler room you'll notice the difference.

968.

When reading a book or ebook, use a clip on LED light instead of main lighting to save power.

969.

A bowl of ice in front of a fan makes a cheap alternative to air conditioning.

970.

Never put hot or warm food in the fridge, it wastes power.

971.

Only run the dishwasher on full to save energy and hot water costs.

972.

If you don't have double glazing, insulation tape for doors and windows is a cheap and effective way of keeping the house warmer.

973.

Use wind up torches instead of battery torches; you will save money on batteries.

974.

Batteries that are about to run out can be given a little bit more life by rubbing them in your hands to warm them and tapping them on a hard surface.

975.

Leave your oven door open after cooking to help heat the room.

976.

Save boiled water in a thermos flask for your next cup of tea; then you don't have to use energy to boil the kettle again.

977.

Bookcases and large items of furniture can help insulate a room; move them to the coldest wall.

978.

Text instead of call, if you're on a pay as you go phone package.

979.

Use AC on an economy setting, if your unit has one.

980.

If you don't have double glazing, you can make your own with clingfilm; this is a cheap and effective method of trapping warm air and keeping drafts out. Instructional videos are available on Youtube.

Health and fitness

981.

Most commercial cold and flu remedies consist mainly of paracetamol and lemon flavouring. Generic paracetamol with some honey and lemon will generally work just as well and is much cheaper.

982.

One part vinegar to four parts water makes a cheap mouthwash. Rinse your mouth out well afterwards with fresh water, as vinegar left in the mouth can erode teeth.

983.

Age spots (liver spots) on the hands can be reduced by dabbing daily with vinegar.

984.

To make one litre of a cheap 'energy drink' mix 900 ml of water with 4 teaspoons of sugar, half a teaspoon of salt and 100 ml of lemon or lime juice.

985.

Overseas opticians are worth checking also for lower costs. Take your prescription on holiday and visit as soon as possible after arrival.

986.

Peppermint tea can sooth stomach upsets and is cheaper than branded medicines.

987.

Rinse toes in vinegar to keep down athlete's foot.

988.

For normal use, cotton handkerchiefs are cheaper than using tissues; but tissues are probably more hygienic if you have a cold.

989.

Save lots of money on dental work by combining a holiday with dentistry. Cities like Budapest in Hungary have English speaking, highly professional dentists who will undertake work for about half the cost of UK dentists.

990.

Save money on throat treatments from the chemist. Half a cup of vinegar, half a cup of water and four teaspoons of honey makes a cough syrup.

991.

Gargling with lemon juice is said to relieve sore throats.

992.

A glass of water with a teaspoon of lemon juice (fresh or from a bottle) makes a cheap and easy 'detox' drink.

993.

Save money on tissues when you have a cold by using soft loo paper instead.

994.

If you don't have aftersun cream, a cold flannel applied to sunburn and regularly changed will keep down inflammation.

995.

A few drops of lavender oil sprinkled on your pillow can act as a sleeping aid.

996.

When you're at the dentist, ask if they have any free samples of toothpaste, floss, mouthwash etc.

997.

Need to lose weight? Turning the heating down can help as the body uses more energy to keep warm, even when you're sitting still. It also saves money.

998.

Cancel gym memberships. Work out at home for free using isometric home exercises which can be found easily online.

999.

A teaspoon of sodium bicarbonate in a glass of water is an economical mouthwash.

1000.

Two tablespoons of Epsom Salts mixed with one cup of water can act as a sunburn relief.

1001.

Five very deep long breaths of fresh air is one of the best stimulants and is absolutely free.

Other frugal living books available from Montpelier Publishing

A Treasury of Thrift: Save Money with Frugal Wisdom from the Past

This book gives you the pick of the advice of the great thrifty writers of the past - including Benjamin Franklin, Samuel Smiles and Lydia Maria Frances Child, author of *The American Frugal Housewife.* This invaluable little book of moneysaving quotations from great writers will help you change your money mindset and help you grow towards financial security with a wealth of thought-provoking ideas that you will want to return to again and again.

Frontier Frugal: Thrifty Hints and Recipes from Times Past

Reduce, reuse and recycle – the nineteenth century way! This book is packed full of helpful hints and recipes from the early 1800s to the early 1900s, when the United States and Canada expanded their frontiers and intrepid pioneers set up frugal, self-reliant homesteads.

The Men's Guide to Frugal Grooming

This book shows how the average man can save over £400 (US$600) per year with easy to follow guidelines. Learn how most male grooming products can be easily substituted with tried and tested, lower-cost alternatives that work just as well. See how to easily and painlessly save money on shaving, shower gels, aftershaves and more!

The Frugal Gentleman: Classic Style for Less Money

This book shows you how to dress well on a budget and how to save money on tailoring as well as off the peg clothing. It also gives advice on maintaining and repairing clothes, so that you can build a great classic and stylish wardrobe for a minimal outlay.

CPSIA information can be obtained at www.ICGtesting.com
Printed in the USA
LVOW08s1047180215

427348LV00031B/1990/P

9 781505 432534